Legal information

© 2023

Author and Editor: M.Eng. Johannes Wild

A94689H39927F

Email: 3dtech@gmx.de

The complete imprint of the book can be found on the last pages!

This work is protected by copyright

Thank you so much for choosing this book!

Table of Contents

Preface

Thank you so much for choosing this book!

You will learn how to use CAD Design software in this book. Guided step by step by the expertise of a German mechanical engineer. Learn everything you need to know about creating 3D objects and how to realize your own ideas and projects, in an easy and comprehensible way! The motivation to write this book was to teach you all important and basic processes of CAD, in a simple (explained with practical examples) and straightforward way. For this purpose, we use a semi-professional CAD software in this course, which you can download for FREE!

Download it here:

https://www.rs-online.com/designspark/mechanical-download-and-installation

This course is especially for beginners and will teach you how to use CAD software and make your own designs. In addition to theoretical explanations on the use of the software and a simple approach to CAD design, you will learn by means of practical and exciting design projects! In this course, you will learn everything you need to know to create three-dimensional components!

Since it is even more fun to be able to materialize your own designs, you can also find beginner's materials and information about how to learn 3D printing in the corresponding book: "3D printing 101: The Ultimate Beginners Guide". Search for it at amazon.com.

1 How to use this Book

Hello and welcome to CAD Design 101!

Thank you very much for choosing this course!

In this course, you will find an introduction to the basics and the operation of CAD design, as well as specific and practical design examples to make the learning process as easy and efficient as possible. As you may already know, the abbreviation CAD stands for "Computer-Aided Design". CAD software is used to create or edit three-dimensional objects. Starting with simple individual parts, through complex parts, up to entire modules that can be virtually assembled.

In this beginner's course, you will learn how the interface of a CAD program is structured and how to make the best use of the individual features to create three-dimensional objects. You will be able to recreate each design project step-by-step and one-by-one, thus gaining an easy introduction to the subject and becoming more familiar with all the functions of a CAD program in the progress.

If you are also interested in 3D printing, you can even materialize the objects afterwards by simply printing them. If you are interested, please enroll in my course: 3D Printing 101 | The ultimate beginner's guide.

The CAD program used in this course is "DesignSpark Mechanical" by RS Components. This program offers a clear and simple user interface and is available for free! The structure of the design features is very similar to the professional and very expensive CAD programs that an engineer or technician uses in his daily work. Download the latest version of DesignSpark Mechanical for free at:

www.rs-online.com/designspark/mechanical-download-and-installation

Professional CAD software licenses such as from "SolidWorks", "Catia", "SolidEdge" or "AutoCAD" and "Inventor" cost one to several thousand dollars and are therefore usually only worthwhile for professional users and freelancers. For this reason, we use the straightforward and free CAD program "DesignSpark Mechanical". The CAD menu is clear and simple, perfect for finding your way around as a beginner. The software offers all necessary commands to create great objects.

If you would like to try other programs, you will find other free software for beginners, advanced and professionals in the following. In some cases, you can only use these programs for simple editing and not for any design itself, as this is the case with some beginner programs. In this course, modelling is explained only by using DesignSpark Mechanical, but since many CAD programs are structured in a very similar way, you will make your way in other CAD programs with ease.

For basic operations and basic designs, you can try TinkerCAD, Meshmixer or 3DSlash.

As this course progresses, you can try FreeCAD or SketchUp.

And for professional applications, Blender and Onshape or even Fusion 360 offer good alternatives.

Beginner	Advanced	Professional
TinkerCAD	DesignSpark	Blender
Meshmixer	FreeCAD	Onshape
3DSlash	SketchUp	Fusion 360

Recommended software highlighted in green!

All popular CAD software works in a very identical way. Let's take a brief look at that now.

2 General Design Principles

To create a 3D model, you must first make a 2D sketch of the desired object. This is done with simple elements, such as: Line, Circle, Rectangle, and Polygon. You can think of making a 2D sketch as drawing in Microsoft Paint. Such a 2D sketch is made on a plane of the three-dimensional space and then transformed into a three-dimensional object using an extrusion command.

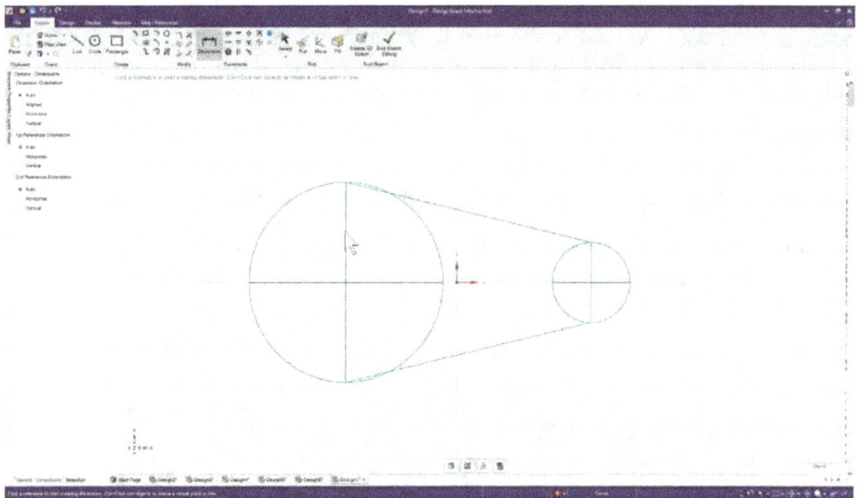

Figure 1: Creating a 2D sketch from basic elements like lines and circles

You will learn exactly how this works in the progress of the course. When approaching 3D objects, there are different methods that vary greatly depending on the designer and the object, but all of them can ultimately lead to the desired result. So, there is not only one way, and you are welcome to think about in which other ways the individual objects could be designed. Sometimes a differing approach will get you easier or faster to the goal, sometimes the opposite is the case. This trains your spatial imagination and is therefore very helpful.

The degree of difficulty of the following chapters and objects increases successively. Therefore, it is best to stay in the order given by the course. With each project, you will learn either a new function or a different way of working. But enough words for the beginning. Let's start with the CAD software! First, a few basics, then we'll get into practical applications.

One more tip on how to use the course: The best and most effective way to learn CAD is to first watch the individual steps carefully, then stop the video after 3-4 steps and try to copy the steps shown without further help. It is best to use this procedure starting with Chapter 3 or alternatively Chapter 5.

In the next sections, we will take a look the interface of the CAD software "DesignSpark Mechanical" and will learn how to create a 2D sketch, as well as the subsequent transfer of the sketch into a 3D object.

Let's get started!

3 The interface and the elements of the CAD software: "DesignSpark"

After starting the program, let's make a few general settings to create the same starting point. Click on "File" in the upper-left corner and then on "DesignSpark-Options".

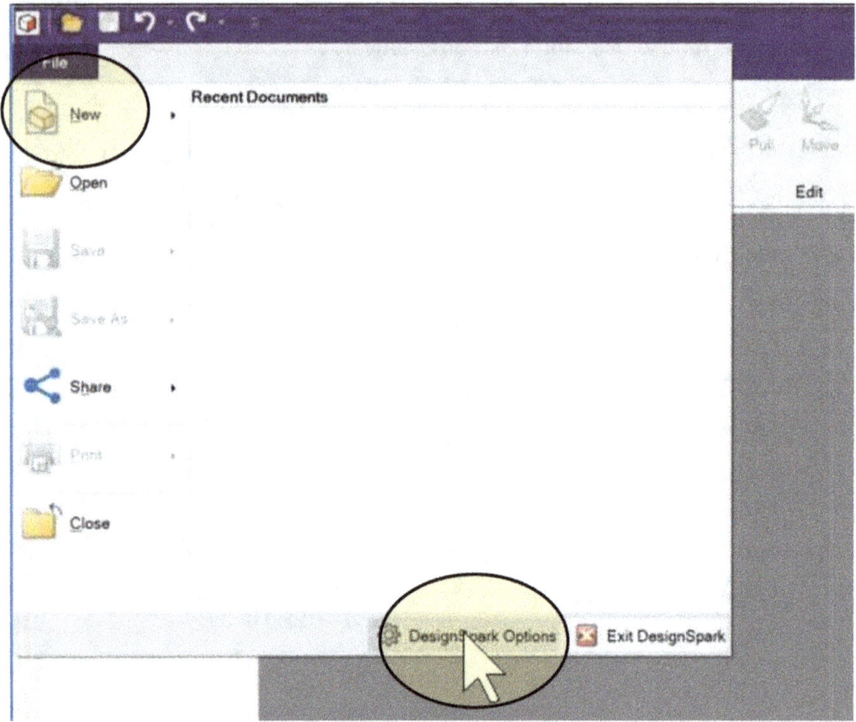

Figure 2: General settings in DesignSpark

It is an advantage to be able to draw as freely as possible. In the menu item "Units" we check the set values. We want to use the metric system and specify length units in millimeters. In addition, angles should be displayed in degrees and masses in grams.

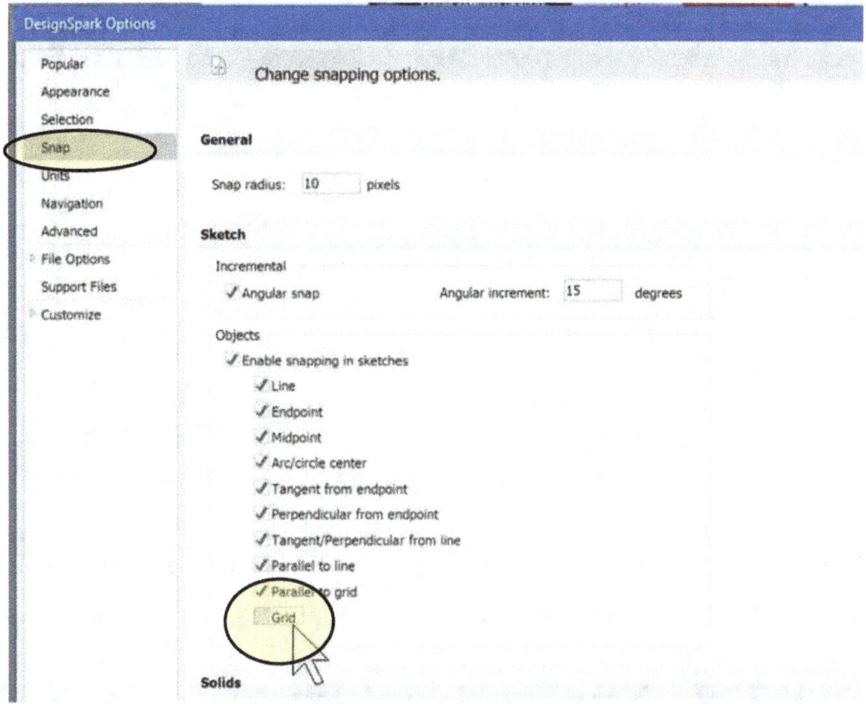

Figure 3: General settings in DesignSpark

In the menu item "Advanced" we activate the topmost setting "Enable constraint based sketching". In this menu item, we can also – if desired – change the language of the menu navigation. If necessary, select your desired language setting at "Language".

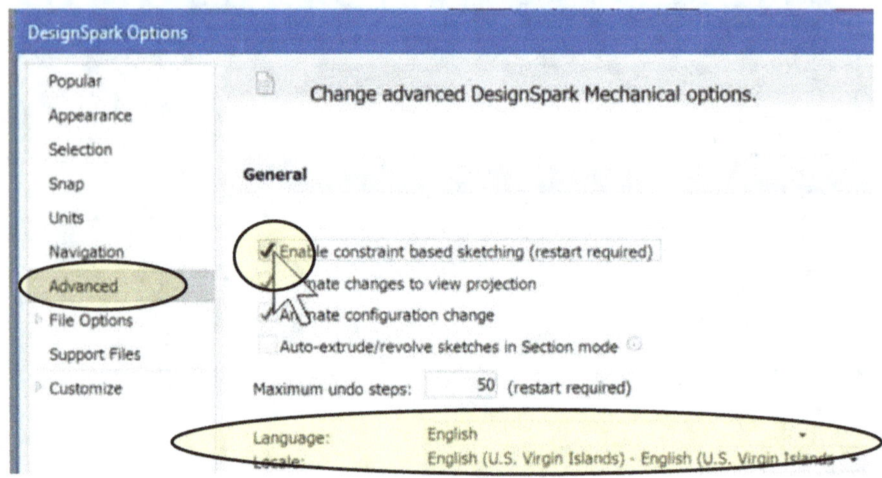

Figure 4: General settings in DesignSpark

Then we exit the settings and restart the program first, to apply all settings. After the restart, we start a new design document by "File" → "New" → "Design"

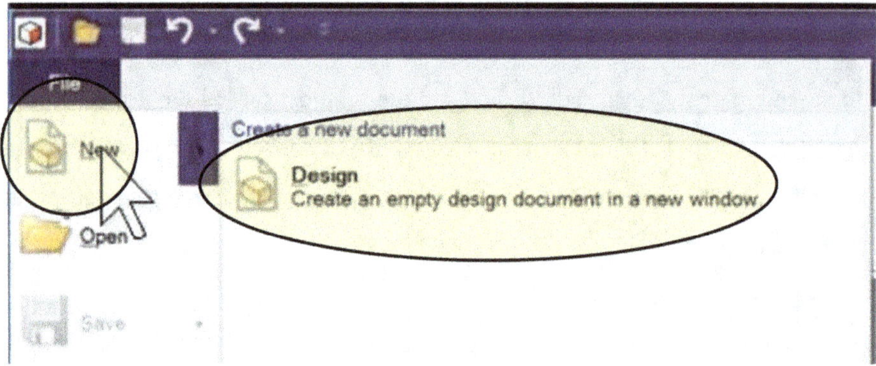

Figure 5: Create a new design document

Let's first take a look at the program environment and the menu bars, which are located in the upper and side areas. We will first deal with the menu section "Design". Here, you can select different views of the component, as well as the basic functions "Pan" and "Spin".

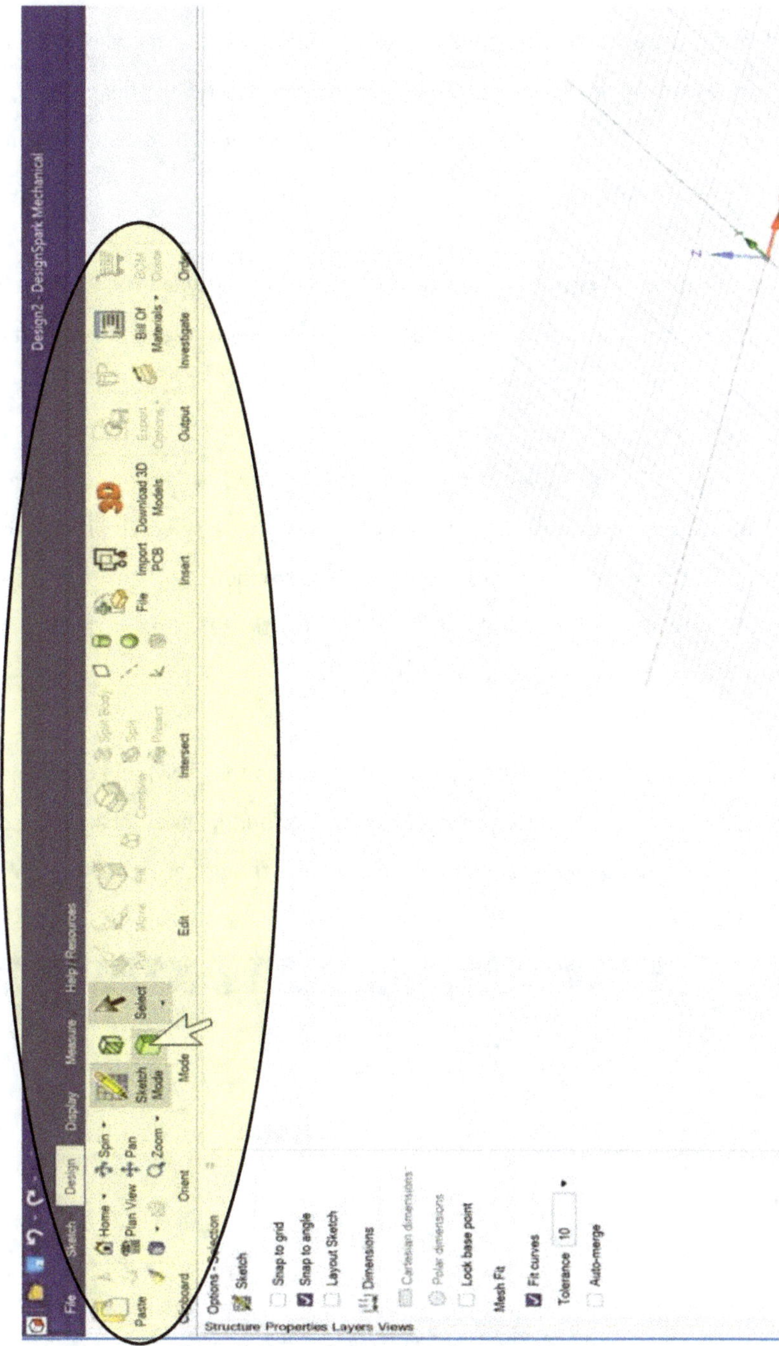

Figure 6: Menu tab design including a lot of functions

Rotating the drawing environment is also possible with the mouse wheel held down while moving the mouse. Shifting is possible with the Shift key pressed, and the mouse wheel pressed. The zoom function is performed as usual by simply turning the mouse wheel.

In the subsequent "Mode" area, it is possible to switch between the 2D sketching mode, the section view and the 3D mode. The "Edit" area offers, in addition to a simple selection tool, functions such as "Pull", "Move" and others. These are relevant when the 3D mode is active.

In the "Intersect" area, bodies or parts can be combined or separated and in the "Insert" area, among other things, planes and axes can be selected or created. In addition, files can be loaded into the design environment or 3D models can be imported from an online database. In the "Investigate" area, the important functions "Measure" and "Dimension" can be found.

In the sidebar on the left, a tree structure, which lists the individual components of a model, as well as the options of commands, are found. The sidebar can also be hidden or rearranged by clicking on the small icon in the upper-right corner of the bar.

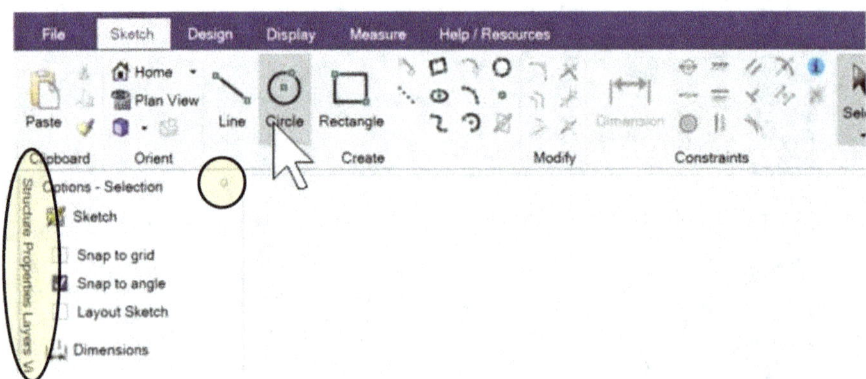

Figure 7: Sidebar of the program

More details about the functions of this bar will be given later in the practical projects.

In the "Sketch" area, the basic elements for creating a sketch, i.e., the two-dimensional drawing with which each object begins, are located. You will need them in 2D sketching mode. Here you can find elements such as: line, circle, arc, rectangle, and others. In addition, edge roundings can be made and conditions such as the "parallelism" of two lines or the "concentricity" of two circles can be defined in the "Modify" and "Constraints" areas. More about this later. We already know "Edit" containing "Pull" and "Move" from the "Design" menu bar, so we can skip those. In the last section: "End Sketch" you can leave the sketch mode after successful editing and switch to the 3D mode.

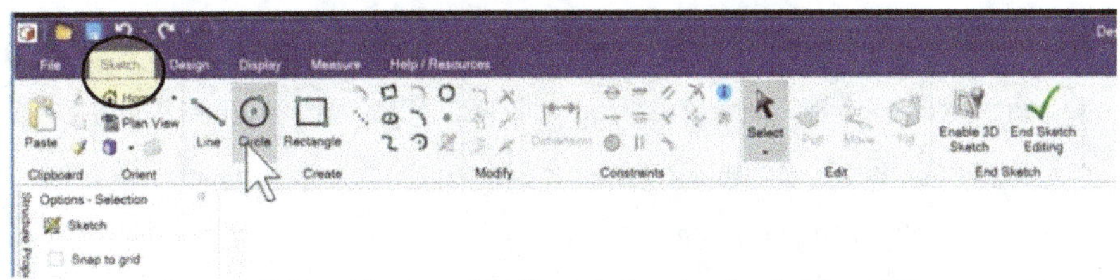

Figure 8: "Sketch" menu tab with various functions for sketch creation

In the next step, we select the menu section "Display". Here, the functions "Paste" and "Views" can be selected again. In addition, the color settings can be changed in the "Style" section and the display of the model can be changed by selecting "Graphics". In the "Window" area, a new window can be opened. In the following area "Grid", settings concerning the sketching grid and the background are to be made. And in the last area "Display" you can select which elements (e.g., the coordinate system) should be displayed or not.

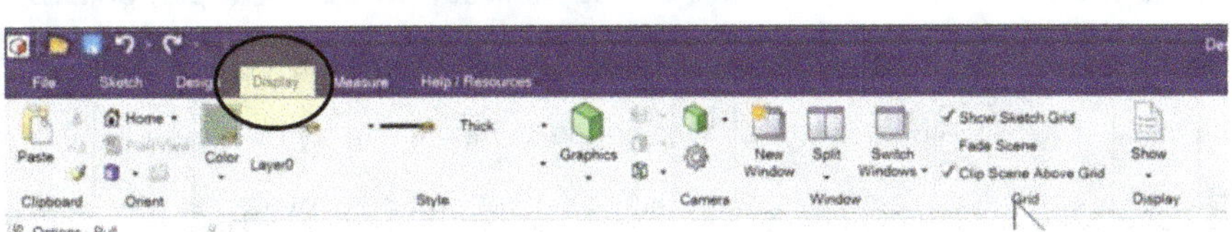

Figure 9: Menu tab "Display" with various functions for displaying

If we switch to the "Measure" tab, once again the dimensioning function represented by a tiny caliper and the possibility to calculate the "Mass Properties" of a component can be found. This feature can be very helpful if you want to determine the weight or the center of gravity of a component.

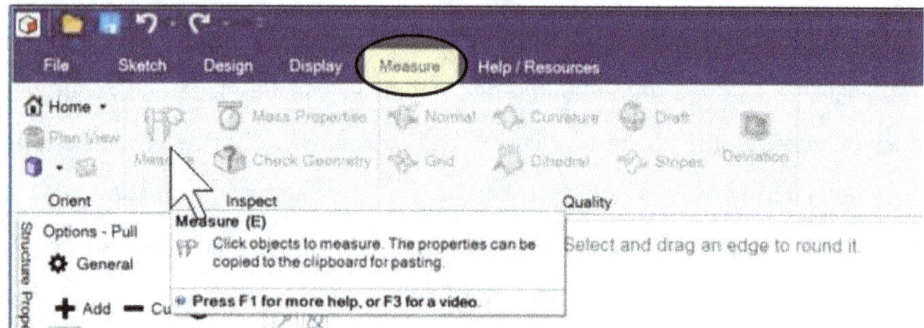

Figure 10: "Measure" menu tab with various functions for dimensioning

In the last menu section, "Help/Resources" tab, you can call up some short guides and tutorials related to the program itself. There is also an interface to the forum and technical support. Thereafter, you will find some sample projects and in the next section you can update. Finally, in the "About" section, you can view general information about the program.

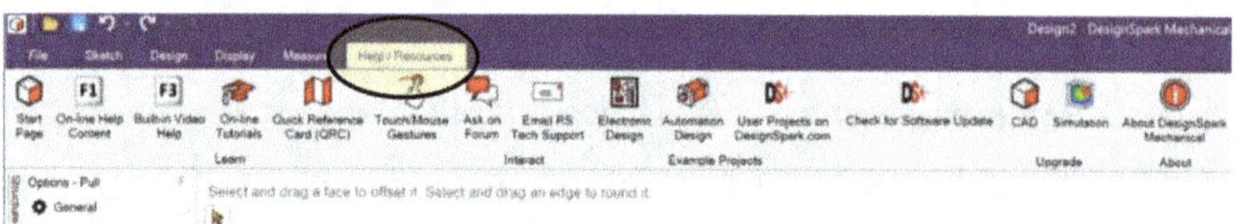

Figure 11: "Help/Resources" menu tab with various help functions

Don't be afraid of the variety of elements and features. We will get to know the individual elements step by step and in detail in this course. Therefore, this brief introduction should be sufficient for the time being.

At the end of this chapter, let's take a closer look at how we can display objects in different views so that we can start directly with the first sketches in the next chapter. If we switch back to the "Design" section, we can try out the selection of the different views. To do this, the 3D mode must first be activated in the "Mode" area. Then, in the "Orient" section, we can choose between numerous views (isometric, trimetric, top, bottom, ...).

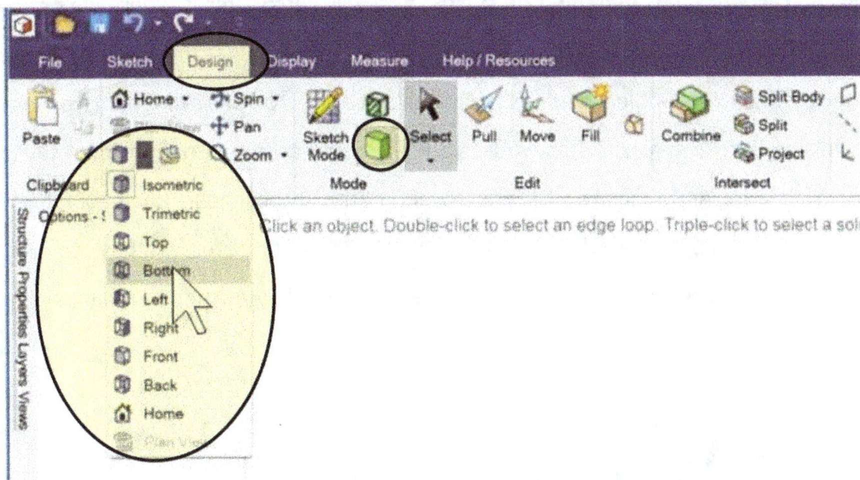

Figure 12: Selection of different views in the "Design" menu tab

And now on to the next chapter, where we are going to learn one of the most basic concepts of CAD: sketching in 2D. Stay tuned!

4 Creating the first 2D sketches

Each 3D component must first be started as a 2D sketch. This is where we define the "blueprint" of the object. Imagine that you are looking at the top of a simple three-dimensional object. Let's assume you look at the top of a cylinder in a perfect right angle to the axis. What would you see? Correct, a two-dimensional circle, nothing else. And starting with this 2D geometry, the cylinder, analogous to all other elements, is created in the CAD software. In the first step, we have to draw the 2D circle. The three-dimensional shape is obtained by further commands.

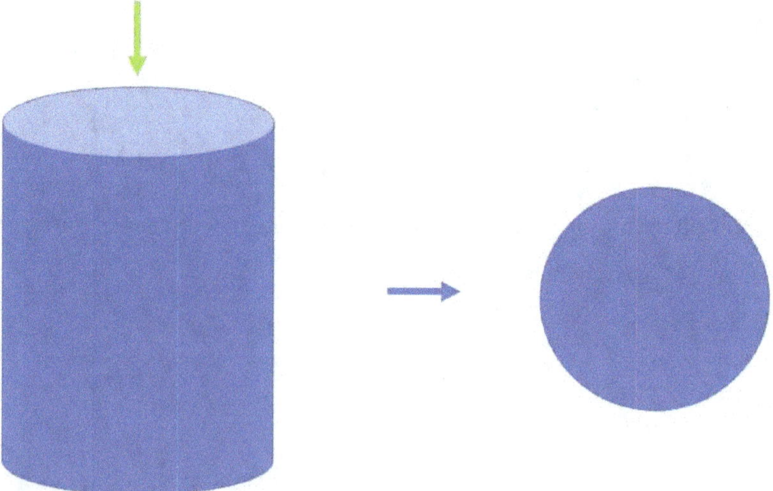

Figure 13: 2D circle as basic shape for a 3D cylinder

At the beginning of a sketch, switch to "Design" and click on the blue z-axis of the small coordinate system or on the plane below it. This will select your sketching plane. In this case, it is the plane spanned by the axes "x" and "y", since we want to look at the top of the final object.

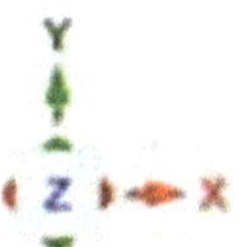

Figure 14: The coordinate system in the lower-left area of the program

First of all, make sure that you are in the "Sketch" mode in the "Design" tab. Always select this "sketch mode" to create a 2D sketch. By selecting it, the program jumps to the "Sketch" tab for selecting geometrical elements.

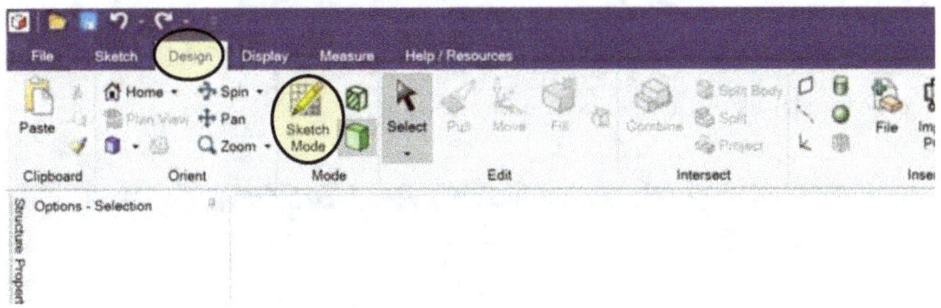

Figure 15: Start "Sketch Mode" in the "Design" menu tab

Before we make the first 2D sketch, uncheck "Show Sketch Grid" in "Display". Then the grid will be suppressed, and you will get the shown display. However, this setting is a matter of taste and does not necessarily have to be made.

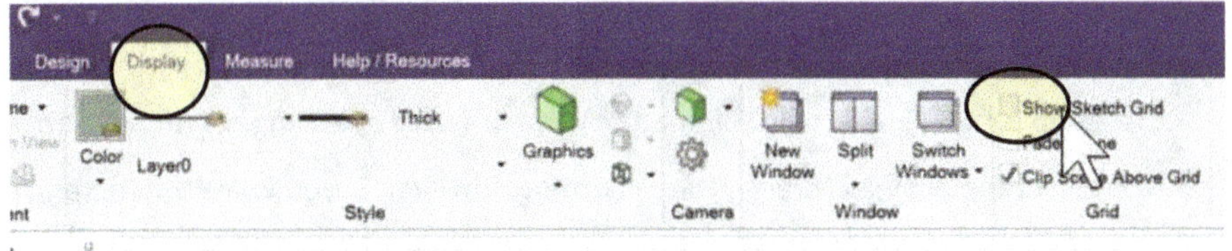

Figure 1: Remove "Show Sketch Grid" in the "Display" menu tab

A variety of basic drawing elements is available for creating a 2D sketch. By selecting "Line", for example, a geometry can be formed from line-shaped elements. Let's try this out. Just click on any point, e.g., in the center of the coordinate system and start drawing by clicking and dragging with your mouse. The drawing should correspond to the cross-section of the desired 3D object or, in the case of simple objects, to the upper surface or cross-sectional area of the object, i.e., a circle as in the case of a cylinder. Also enter the desired dimensions with the help of your keyboard.

Besides a line, you can also create a circle, an ellipse, a curve, or a rectangle. Let's try them.

In the "Sketch" panel you will also find: a point, various arcs and several other elements.

It is best to try all the elements at least once.

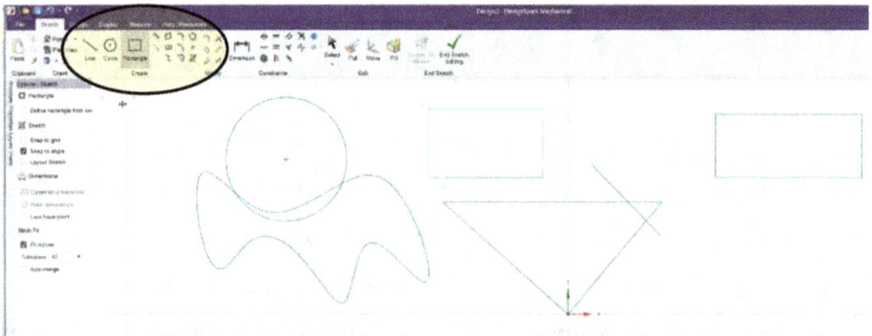

Figure 2: Sketching exercises with line, circle, rectangle, etc.

Another tip for the "Rectangle" element: When drawing a rectangle, you will notice that the rectangle always starts from a corner. However, if you want the rectangle to span from the center, you can make the very helpful setting "Define Rectangle from Center" in the sidebar at "Properties". This setting option is also available for other elements.

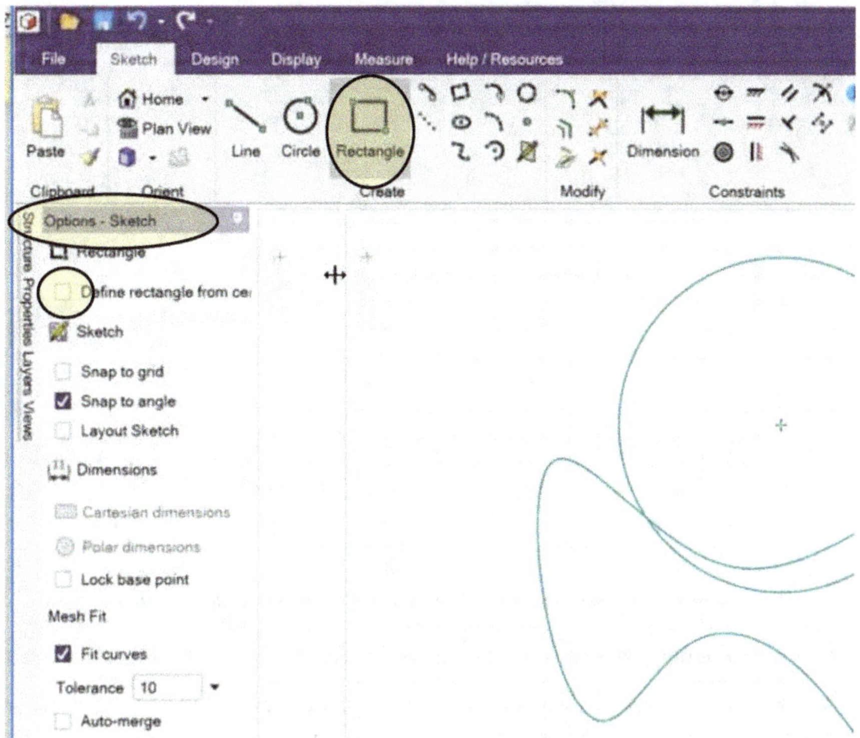

Figure 3: Create a rectangle or another geometry element from the center point

To finish these simple 2D sketching exercises, please draw a rectangle, which you can then provide with fictitious dimensions using "Dimension". For example, select a width of 35 mm and a height of 20 mm. To do this, click on "Dimension" and then on the desired line. There are two ways leading to the goal: You can draw a rectangle with the correct dimensions by already entering the values using your keyboard while drawing. A tip: Use the tabulator key to switch between the individual fields for entering the dimensions. Alternatively, you can first draw a random rectangle and later change the dimensions. You can do this by double-clicking on the dimension. Then enter the desired value and confirm with Enter.

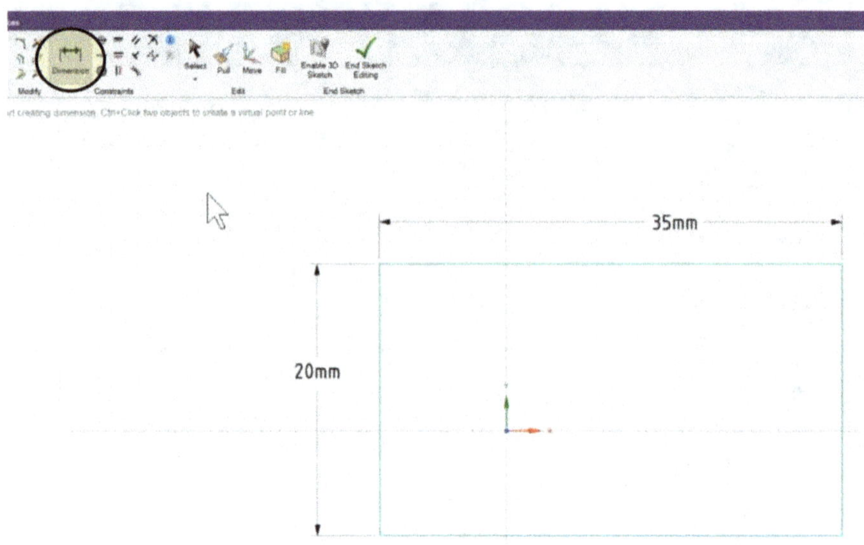

Figure 4: Draw a rectangle and dimension it with the "Dimension" function

You can also dimension the distance between two lines. To do so, just click on the first line and then on the second line whose distance you want to dimension. "Dimension" must be active. Now it's your turn! Pause the video briefly and try to draw a rectangle with the given dimensions.

You can end the sketching mode with the green tick in the upper menu bar. In the lower area, you will also find some helpful buttons to exit the sketch mode. Select the small green cube and the program will exit sketching mode and then automatically switch to 3D mode. You can also use the other buttons to select a new sketching layer or move the grid.

Figure 5: Buttons for various functions in the lower area

To create a three-dimensional object, it is important that the sketched element is completely closed and does not have any gaps. This is indicated by a green background, that fills the sketched element. It means that the surface has a continuous boundary line without gaps.

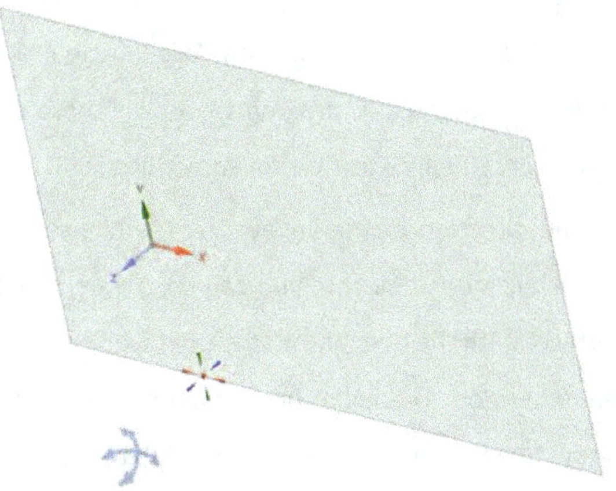

Figure 6: Sketched area in 3D mode (green background)

After selecting 3D mode, rotate the environment by keeping the mouse wheel pressed while moving the mouse or by using the coordinate system located at bottom left. Then select "Pull" and click on the area of the rectangle. In the upper-left corner, you will see more options for the "Pull" function. But more about that later.

In the next chapter, we will create a three-dimensional object from the 2D sketch. Great, you are making good progress! We will get to the first project soon!

5 Creating a three-dimensional object from a 2D sketch

As announced, we want to create a 3D object from the 2D sketch. For this, we need to use the previously selected "Pull" function. This function represents a so-called extrusion command. In other CAD programs, you will therefore often find terms such as "Extrusion" or "Linear Extrusion" or something similar.

If you move in the direction of the yellow arrow while selecting the "Pull" and holding down the left mouse button, you can create a three-dimensional object from the 2D surface. With the help of the space bar, you can pause the process and enter a desired dimension. Then confirm with Enter. The "Pull" function is a very basic and versatile function, as we will see in the following.

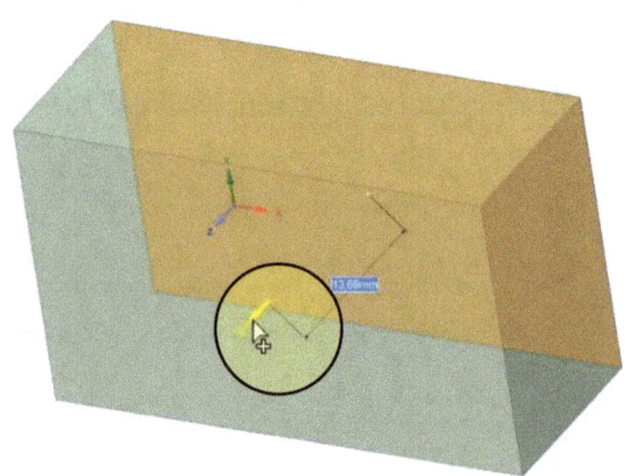

Figure 7: The 2D surface is transformed into a 3D body with "Pull"

Since this three-dimensional object is relatively simple, we want to further modify the object to learn a few basic operations in 3D mode. One possible approach to design is to work in the same way that actual machining – milling or turning, for example – would be done. You first create the raw material, in this case the cuboid, and then machine it successively in further steps – using cutouts, holes, and other design features to get the final object. That is why this type of designing is called subtractive. You reduce the initial material through individual processing steps until the desired object is obtained. There are also other approaches, such as the additive variant. In this case, the CAD model or even the real object – as is the case, for example, with 3D printing – is built up element by element.

However, we will first deal with the conventional subtractive approach. In the next steps, we want to make a drilling and a rectangular cutout into our object. To do this, we first need to make a 2D sketch of the geometries for the hole and the cutout. To do this, click on "Sketch Mode" and select the top face of the cuboid, since we want to drill the hole into the cuboid from top to bottom. The top face of the cuboid in this case is the face that is parallel to the x-y plane in the z direction, since the cuboid has been rotated as shown here.

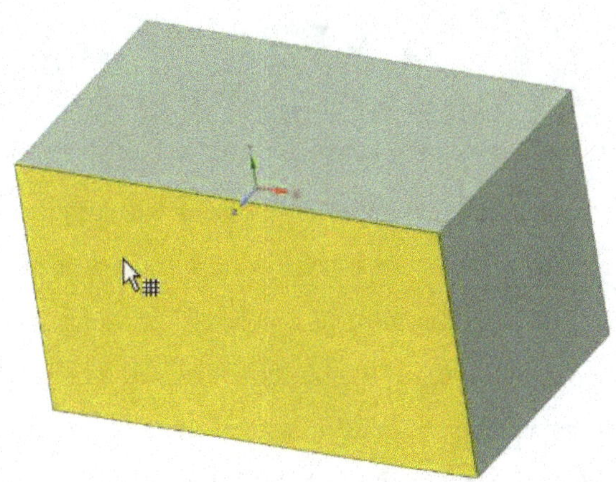

Figure 8: With this orientation, the plane between x and y is the top

Then select "Top" or navigate with the small coordinate system from the bottom. We now want to drill the hole. Select the option "Circle" for creating the 2D geometry.

Then place the circle on the surface with a click and enter a diameter of e.g., 4 mm. Confirm with "Enter". Next, we define the position of the circle using "Dimension". Since we are in two-dimensional space, i.e., sketching on a parallel of the x-y plane, we need an x- and a y-dimension to completely define the sketch or the circle. Enter the desired dimensions: e.g., 5 mm each from the left and upper edge of the cuboid. Now the circle for the hole is completely dimensioned. It has a defined diameter and dimensions in x- and y-axis direction to defined points. A complete dimensioning and a completely defined sketch is very important for good results, always pay attention to it.

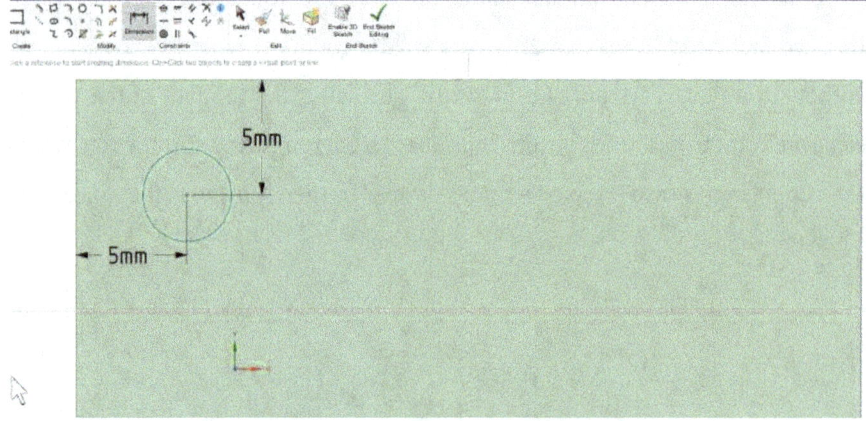

Figure 9: Creating and dimensioning the circular geometry for the hole

We also want to create the geometry for the rectangle cutout in this editing step, since we are already on the correct layer – the surface of the cuboid. To do this, first sketch a construction line, which is simply a sort of guide line, from the center of the top edge to the center of the bottom edge of the rectangle. We need this for easier positioning. Then select the rectangle and place it in the center using "Dimension". We need half a side length here, which results in a dimension of 2.5 mm. The dimensions of the rectangle should be 5 mm each, to get a square.

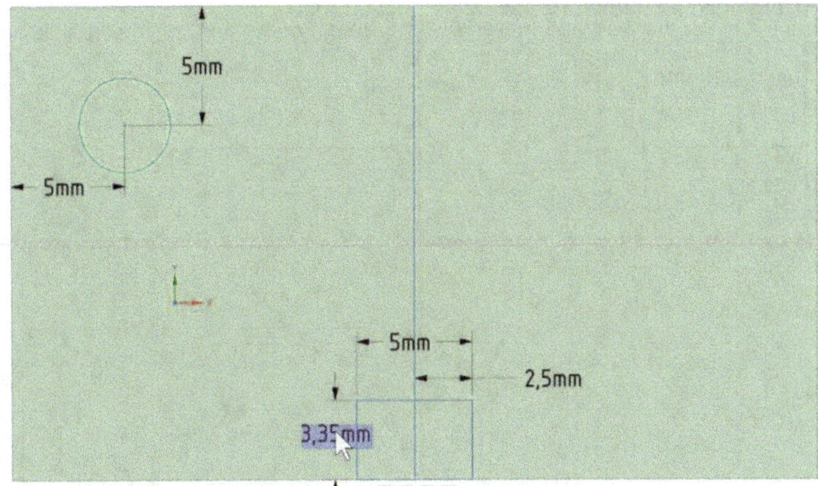

Figure 10: Create and dimension the rectangle geometry for the cutout

Exit the sketch mode or switch to 3D mode and rotate the object with your mouse. Then select "Pull" and click on the surfaces of the two sketched geometries. Move them by holding down the mouse button and dragging in negative z-axis direction, i.e., in the direction of the interior of the cuboid.

As you can see, the drilling and the cutout are created. Use the space bar to pause the process and enter the desired dimension.

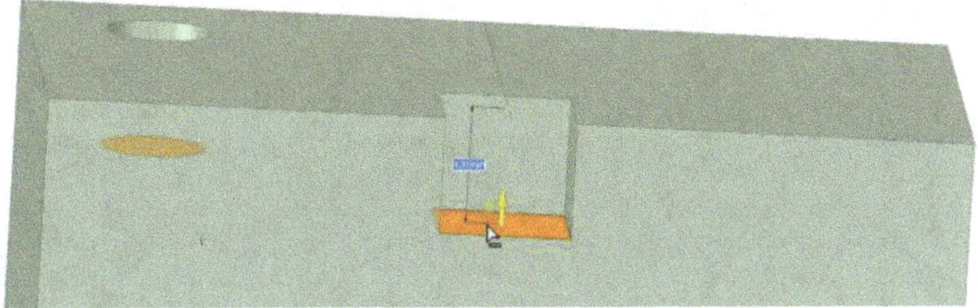

Figure 11: Creating the hole and the cutout in 3D mode

With the "Pull" function, it is also possible to add material instead of removing it, as was already seen during the creation of the cuboid. To do this, you only have to move your cursor in the opposite direction or select "Add" in the sidebar at "Options – Pull". Here, you can switch between "Add" and "Cut". You can use the option "Add" when designing using an additive approach. This is the case, whenever you want to add material to an object instead of removing it through virtual machining.

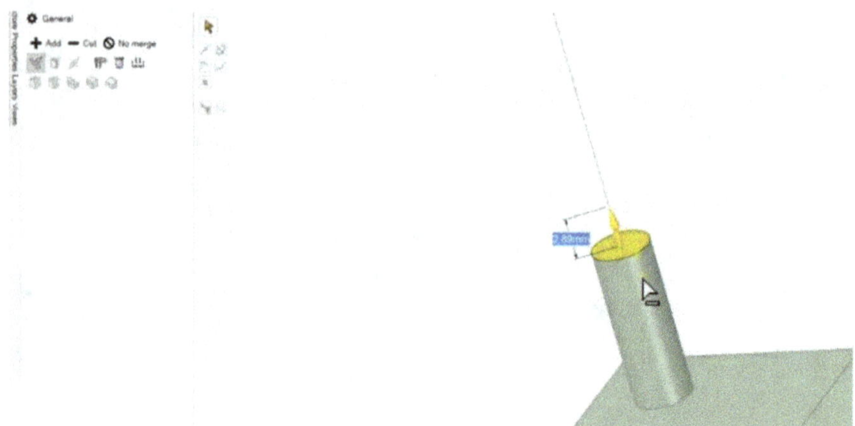

Figure 12: "Options-Pull" in the left sidebar with "Add" and "Cut"

Similarly, the "Pull" feature allows you to round edges or create chamfers. For this feature, first select the desired edge or multiple edges. Select multiple edges by holding down the CTRL key. Then move the cursor in the direction of the arrow and use the space bar to specify the desired dimension, i.e., the radius. Alternatively, just click on the edge again, and you can edit the radius.

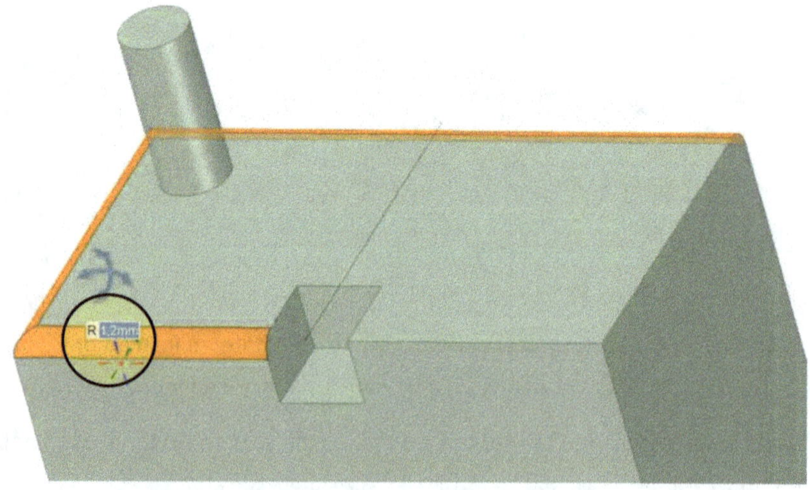

Figure 13: Rounding of edges by using the "Pull" function

As you can see, "Pull" is very powerful and offers a variety of basic editing options. To conclude this chapter, we will get to know one more function in 3D mode. With "Shell" you can easily hollow out an object. To do this, select the function and the bottom surface of the object.

That's it, the object is hollowed out. The desired wall thickness can be entered using the space bar and the keyboard. Pretty simple, isn't it?

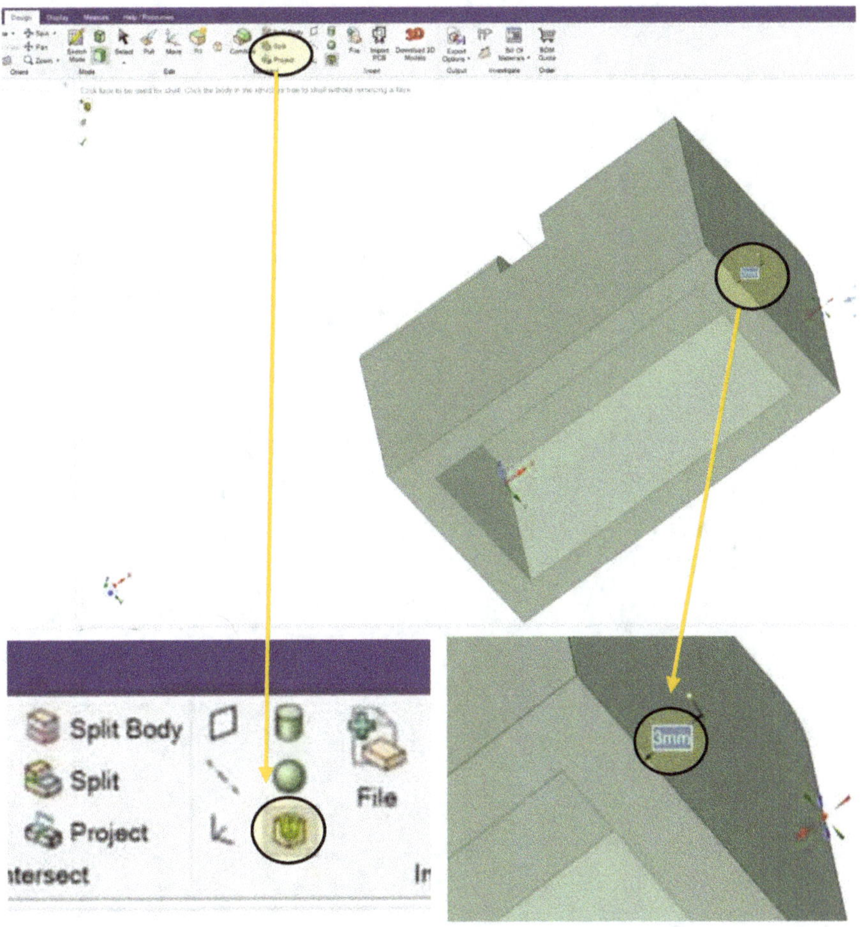

Now you already know how to create a two-dimensional sketch and generate a 3D object from it. You also know the design environments in two- and three-dimensional space and the most important functions of these. This means, that we know all the necessary basics and are now ready to start with the actual design projects. In the following chapter, we'll first design a practical clothing hook, which you can attach to a door frame. Here we go!

6 Design Project # I: Hook

6.1 Designing a hook

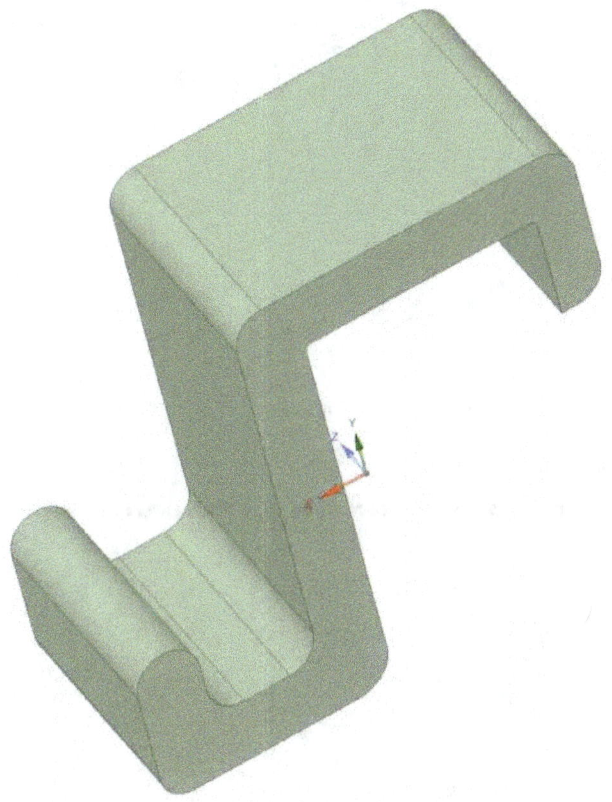

This hook has a quite simple geometry. For this object, it is recommended to draw the cross-section of the model in 2D and then use the "Pull" function to make it three-dimensional. First, we draw the cross-section of the hook. Start by selecting the "2D sketch mode" and continue by selecting the z-axis or the x-y plane and then draw the first line, as shown.

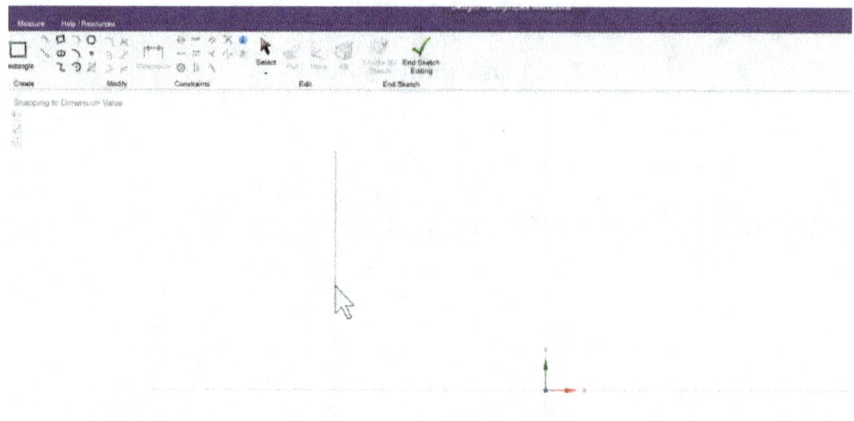

Figure 14: Start with a vertical line 11 mm long

Then, add the following lines and dimensions:

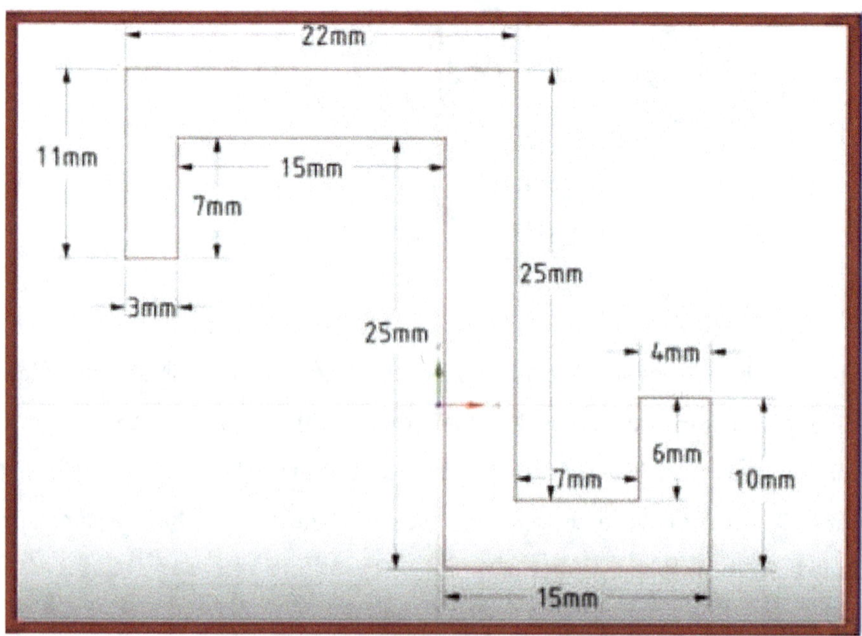

Figure 15: Add the following lines to complete the profile

Then you can leave the 2D sketching environment and switch to 3D mode. Select "Pull" and create a three-dimensional body by dragging in the direction of the displayed arrow. Enter a dimension of 15 mm by using your keyboard.

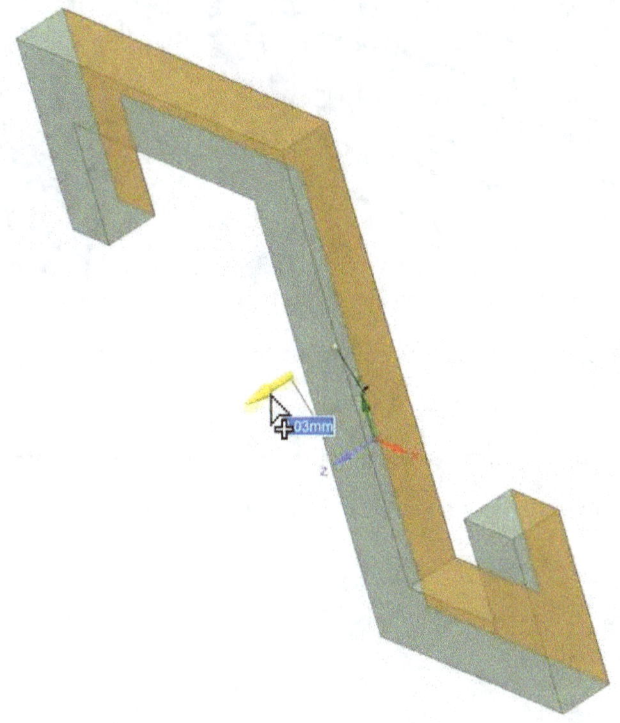

Figure 16: Start with a vertical line 11 mm long

Up to this step, you could of course also use the subtractive design method. Let's try it.

To do this, we will draw a rectangle with 33 mm and 29 mm in the 2D sketch mode and create a cuboid with a thickness of 15 mm using "Pull".

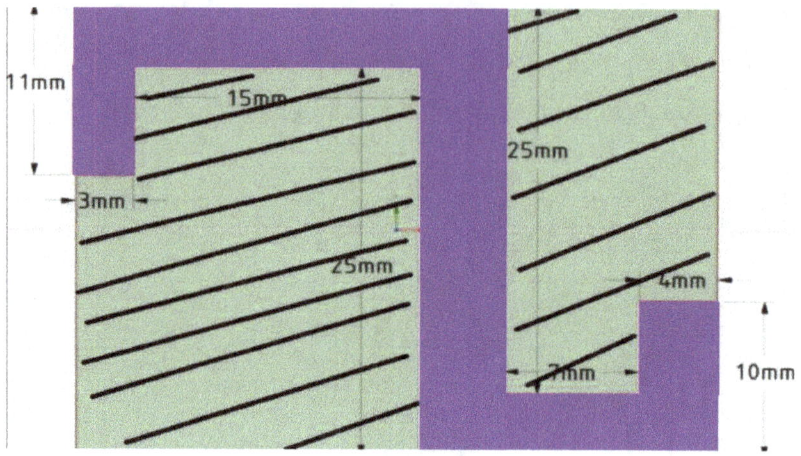

Figure 17: Hatched areas of the box (green) should be cut away

Note: The program automatically switches to 3D mode, when selecting "Pull". Usually, we would click on End 2D Sketch at this point.

Next, we draw the sketches for the cutouts. To do this, we first create a 2D sketch on the top – alternatively, of course, the bottom – surface.

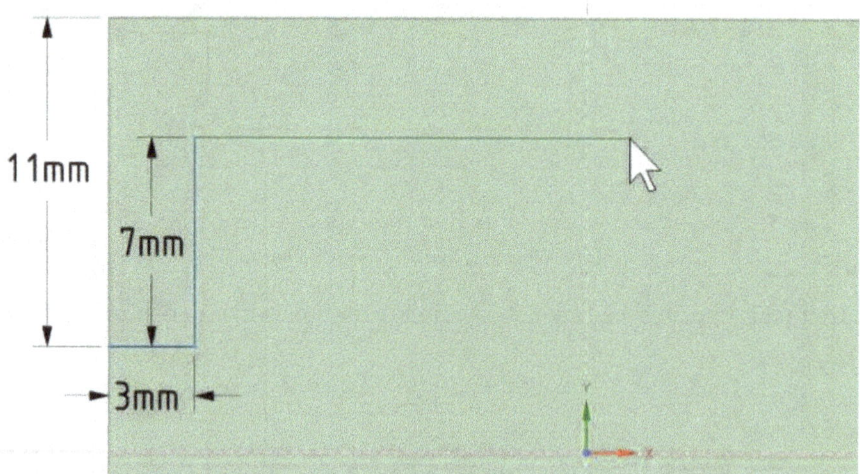

Figure 18: Sketch the depicted lines on the created cuboid
(top or bottom of the cuboid)

First, sketch the left half of the cutout for the hook. And then the right half. Also make sure that there are two closed surfaces for the cutouts, i.e., that you connect the lines at the edges of the cuboid surface.

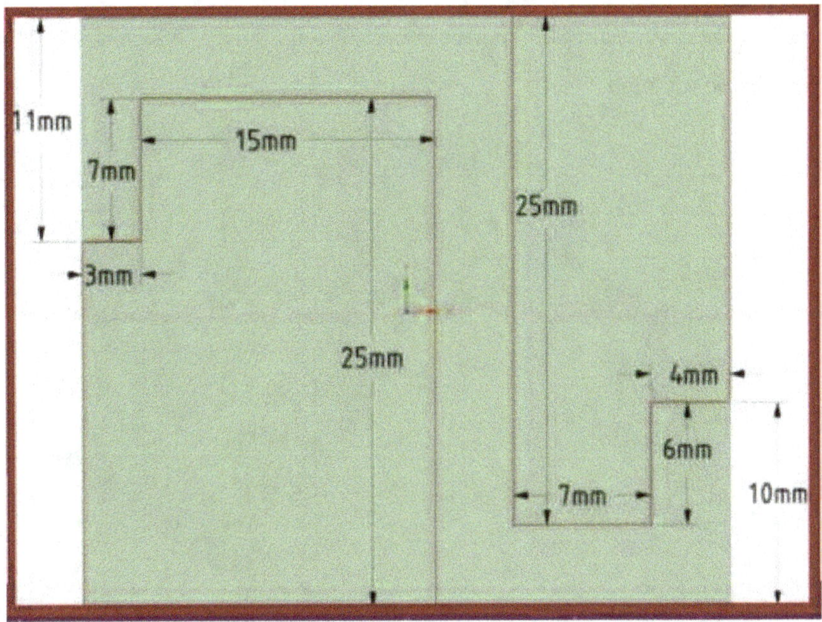

Figure 19: Sketch the red lines shown

Thereafter, you can use "Pull" to cut out the sketched areas. Two approaches for an identical solution.

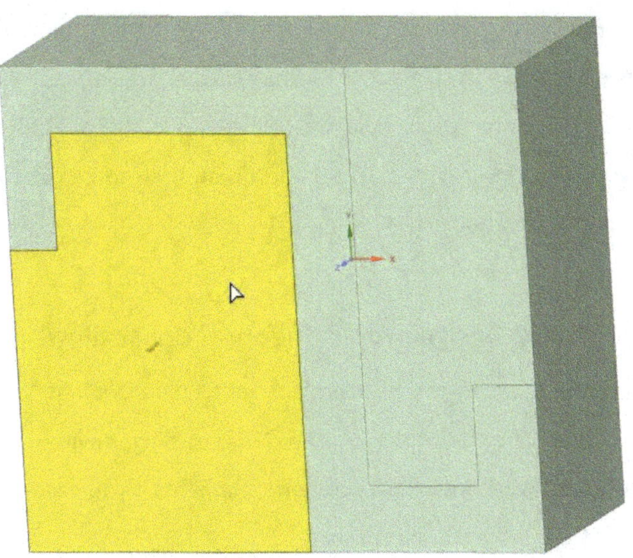

Figure 20: Cut away the material that is not needed

Finally, in 3D mode, we can do some edge rounding. Select all the desired edges using the CTRL key. With "Pull" and selection of "Rounding" in "Options – Pull" the edges can be rounded.

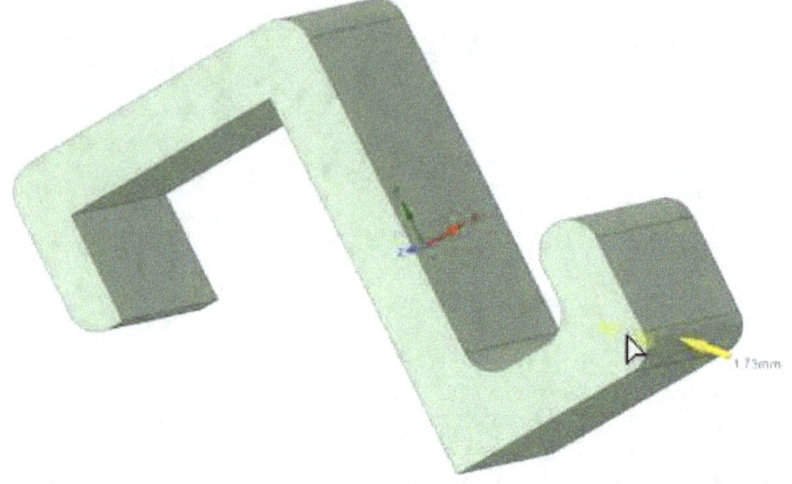

Figure 21: Rounding of some edges

For example, use a radius of R = 2 mm and R = 1 mm, or at your own discretion.

Perfect! Then the hook is done and can be saved. Select the desired file type by choosing "File" and "Save as". If you want to edit the project later on, it is recommended to save the file as "DS Mechanical file". If you would like to print the object with a 3D printer, you should also select the file format ".stl". After slicing a "gocde" you can print it with a 3D printer. If you wish to know more about 3D-Printing, consider my book: 3D Printing 101.

6.2 Design project theory : "Constraints"

Great! Before we get to the next project, let's take a look at "constraints", or conditions. You can use these in the 2D sketching environment to create dependencies between individual geometric elements if you need to.

Figure 22: "Constraints" in the menu tab "Sketch"

In the following, we will take a closer look at the most important "constraints". Let's start with the horizontal and vertical ones. Suppose we try to draw a rectangle by using lines, but instead get such a polygon.

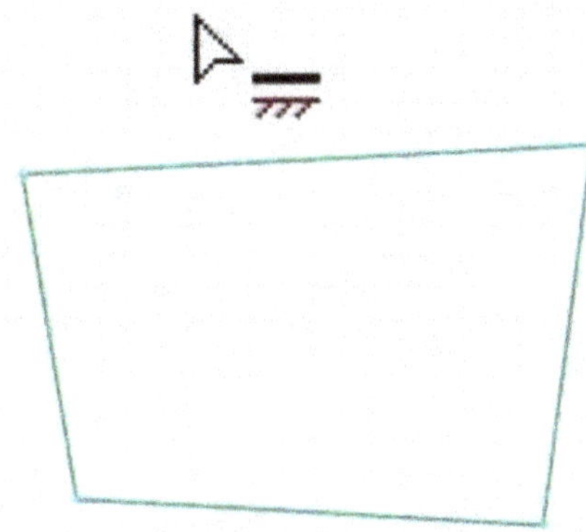

Figure 23: Turn a polygon into a rectangle

By selecting the "horizontal" condition, we will get two perfectly horizontal lines. Just by clicking on the respective lines.

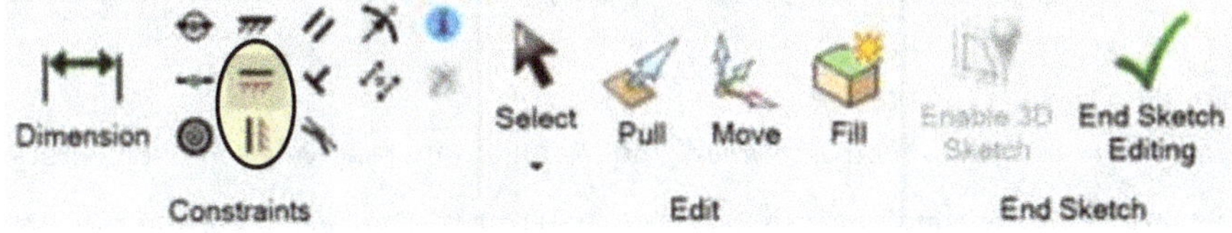

Figure 24: Select "Parallel" or "Vertical" constraint

In the same way, we apply the "vertical" condition to the lateral lines and, finally, get a rectangle. Of course, we would have reached our goal more easily if we had used the predefined element for a rectangle right away, but to illustrate these two "constraints" we took the laborious way.

With "concentric" two circle structures can be set concentric to each other. To do so, let's draw a large circle and a slightly smaller one. We want to get two concentric circles, i.e., two circles with congruent axes. We accomplish this by selecting the appropriate constraint and the two circle.

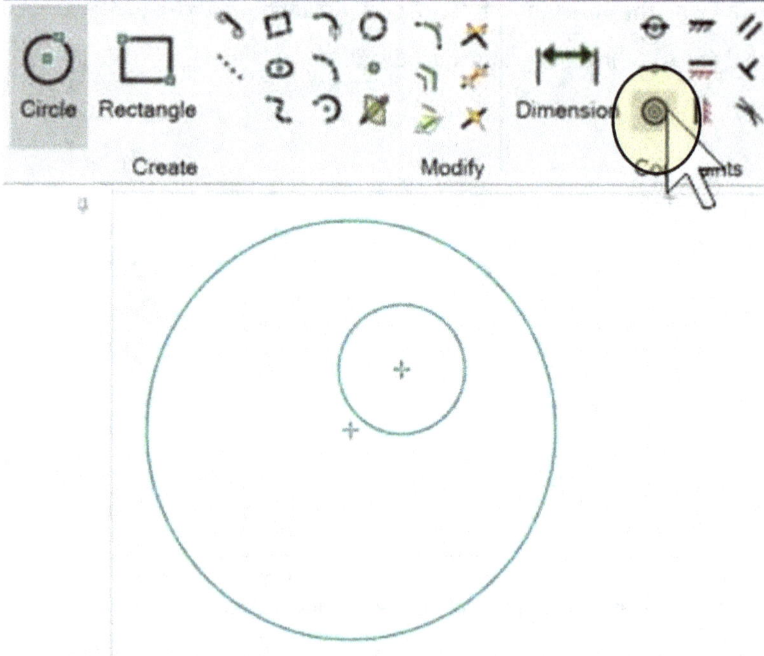

Figure 25: Select the constraint "Concentric" and click on the two circles

The two constraints: "Perpendicular" and "Parallel" are relatively self-explanatory. Nevertheless, let's look at a small example with two lines each. For the function "Perpendicular" we draw the following two lines. By choosing the condition and selecting the lines, we get two lines that are perpendicular to each other.

Figure 26: Perpendicular and parallel constraints

For "Parallel" we draw two more lines and by selecting the condition we get two lines perfectly parallel to each other.

The "Constraints": "Coincident" and "Midpoint", you should use whenever you want to connect two points or connect a point of one element with the midpoint of another element. Let's draw a rectangle and two lines to illustrate this.

We would like to connect the first line with a corner point of the rectangle and the second line with the center of one of the lines of the rectangle.

By the way, you can also apply multiple "constraints". For example, we could also apply the constraint horizontally to this line.

Let's have a look at the "Tangent". As the name and the small picture already indicate, we can use it to set a line tangent to a circle, for example. Let's try it. First draw the circle, then a line and then apply the constraint.

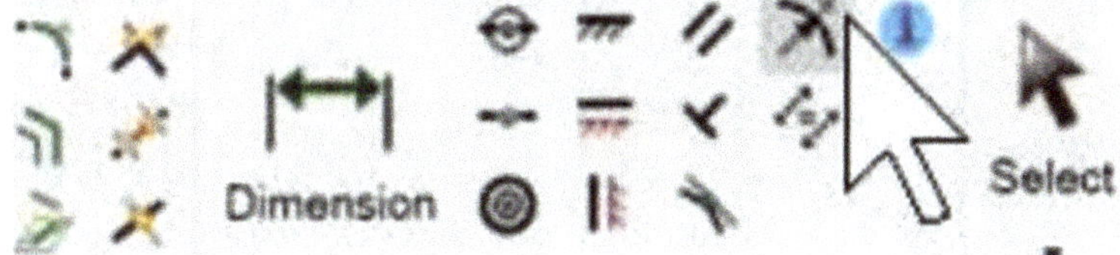

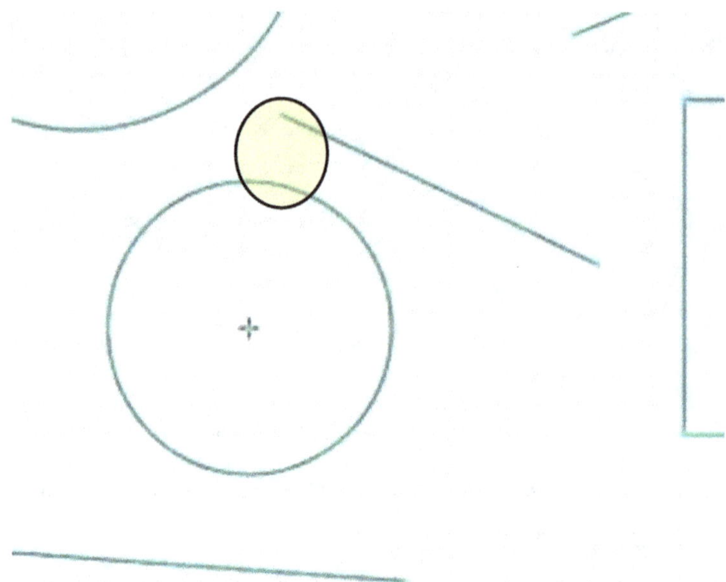

Figure 27: Applying the constraint: "tangent"

You are welcome to try the 3 remaining constraints: "Fixed", "Equal Radius" and "Equal Distance" yourself, as the name is relatively self-explanatory. "Fixed" simply fixes an element in the drawing plane and the other two provide equal radius or equal distance between elements. Just try it!

That's it for this theoretical section at the end of the chapter. In the next chapter, we will start a new project: You will learn how to design a simple carabiner. Stay tuned, it will be worth it! With each chapter, the projects will get a little more complex and exciting!

7 Design Project # II: Snap Hook

7.1 Designing a snap hook

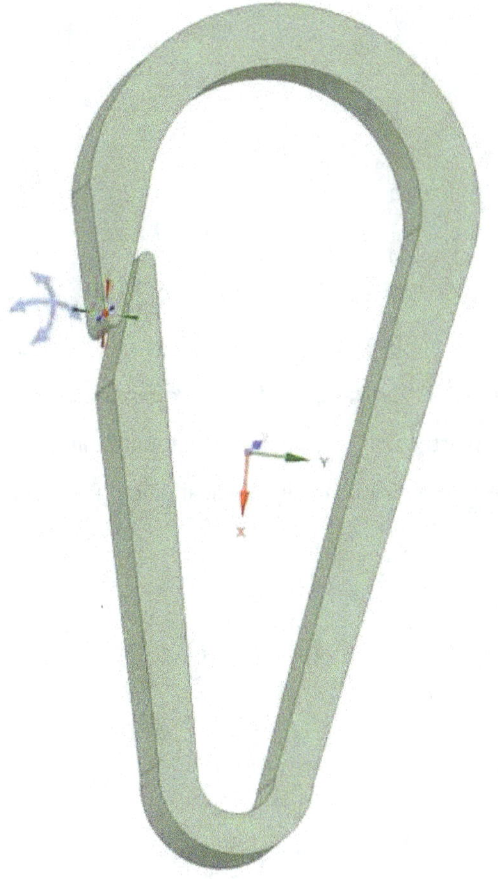

We will start a new project for the snap hook in 2D sketching mode and select a plane. Let's first consider how the snap hook is structured and how we could design it. If we take a little closer look, you will notice a circular shape in the left and the right area, as well as struts for tangential connections between these circles. Let's try to do it this way.

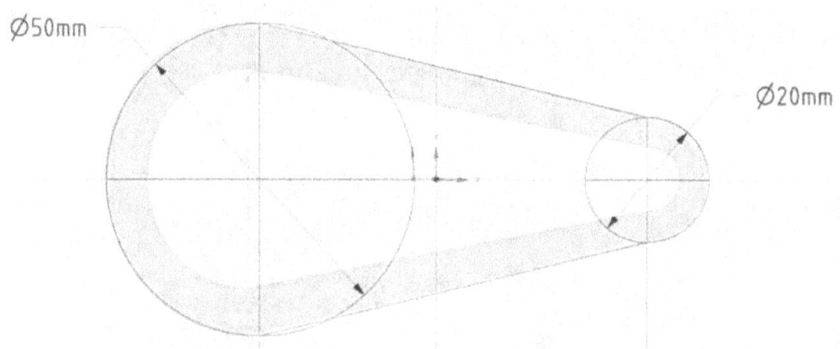

Figure 28: Carabiner geometry

First, simply draw a circle. E.g., with a diameter of 50 mm, e.g., on the x-y plane.

Then, create another circle with a diameter of 20 mm next to the first one. Next, we draw horizontal and vertical guide lines through the centers of the two circles to make it easier to attach dimensions and the tangent lines. In the next step, let's connect the intersection points of the vertical guide lines with the circles by two more lines.

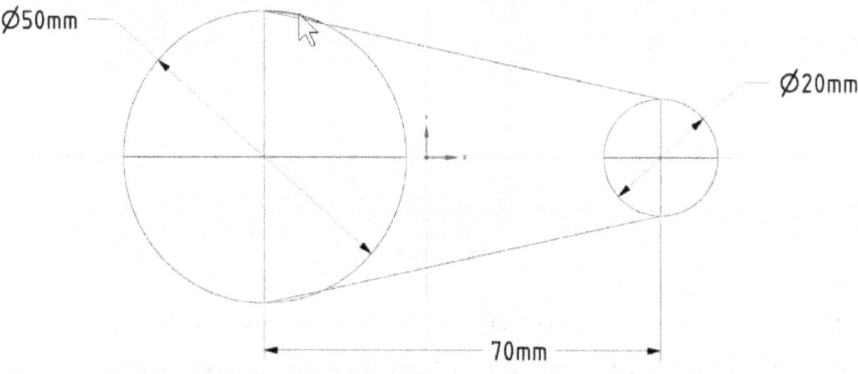

Figure 29: Creating the 2D sketch for the snap hook

To get a closed shape, we only need the outer contour. Therefore, we use the "Trim away" tool.

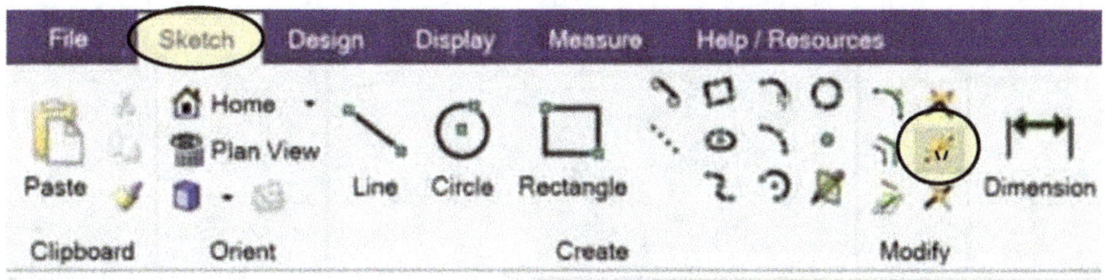

Figure 30: Trim away tool from the Modify section in Sketch

Using this tool, remove all superfluous line segments (just click on the lines) to get a shape as follows:

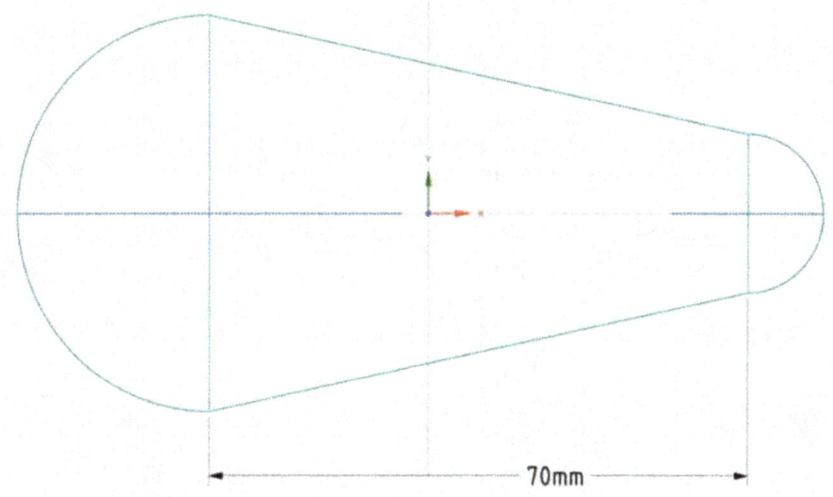

Figure 31: All superfluous lines are now removed

Now we could extrude the surface. But then we would have to make a cut-out in the following step to get the final snap hook shape. However, now that we are a bit more advanced, we might as well use a faster solution and draw the full cross-section of the snap hook in one step.

To achieve this, add two additional circles with diameters of 35 and 10 mm to the inside of the snap hook and again draw two lines from the intersection points of the circles with the auxiliary lines.

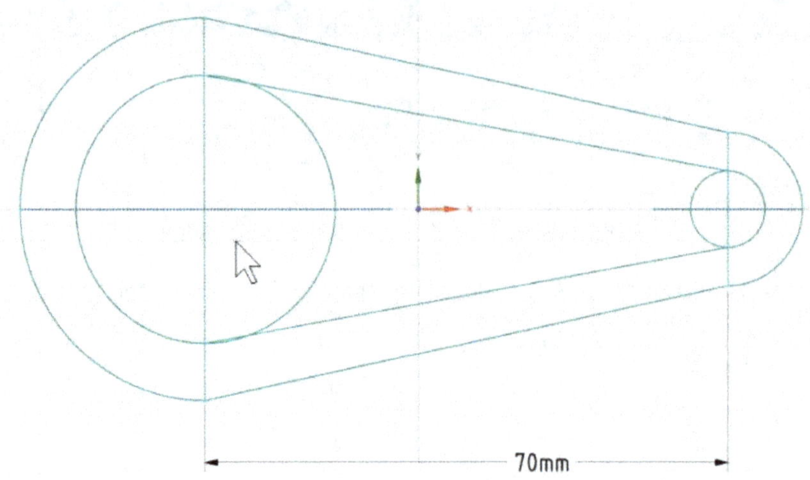

Figure 32: Completing geometry with two circles and tangential lines

Finally, remove all superfluous line segments by using the "Trim away" feature.

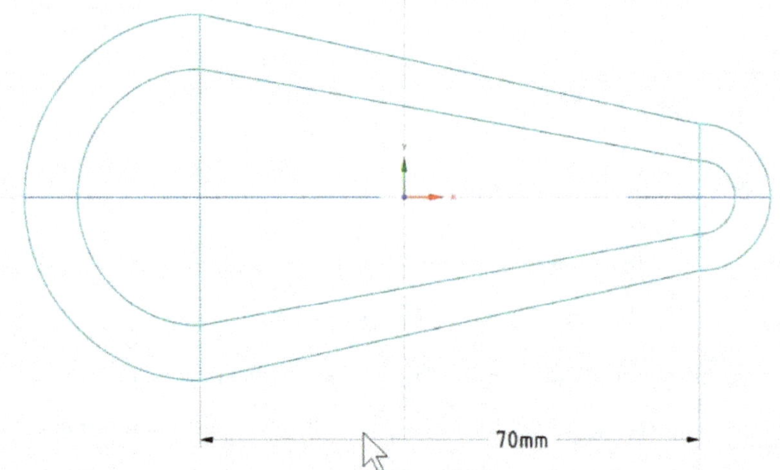

Figure 33: All superfluous line segments removed

As you can see, this saves one editing step, and we can now extrude the shape of the carabiner.

To do this, we switch to 3D mode once more and use the "Pull" function. Select the outer surface of the snap hook and enter a value of 10 mm.

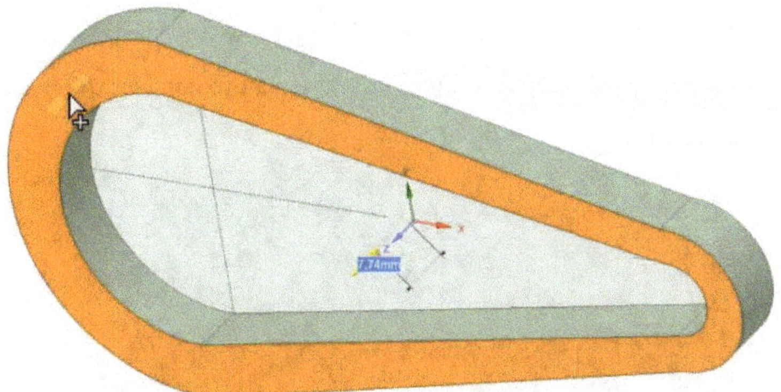

Figure 34: Creating the three-dimensional geometry

You can remove the surface in the middle of the carabiner by right-clicking on it and selecting "Delete".

Now, to create a section for opening the hook, we switch to 2D mode and draw a line at 20° from the intersection of the guide line with the carabiner to the outer line of the carabiner. The dimension is calculated automatically by specifying the angle and the end points.

Then draw a second parallel line with a distance of 2 mm. Of course, we could have also integrated this step into the first sketch, as you may have just noticed.

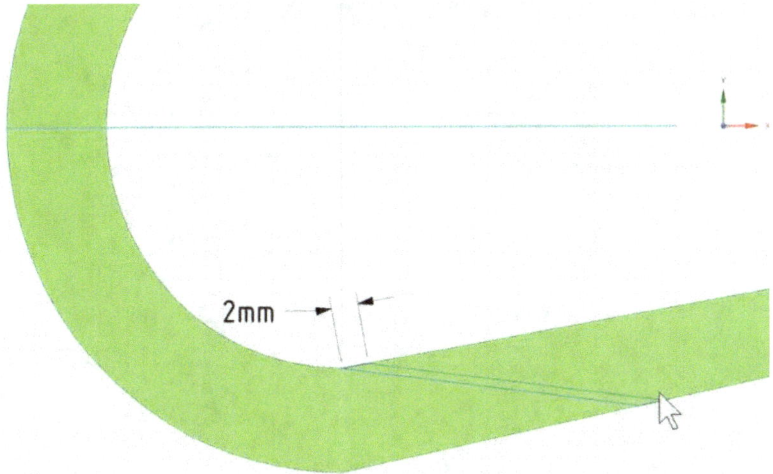

Figure 35: Creating two parallel lines for the cutout

In 3D mode, we can then select the area and drag it towards the snap hook so that this area is cut out and a gap is formed. Do not forget to connect the two lines to form a closed surface.

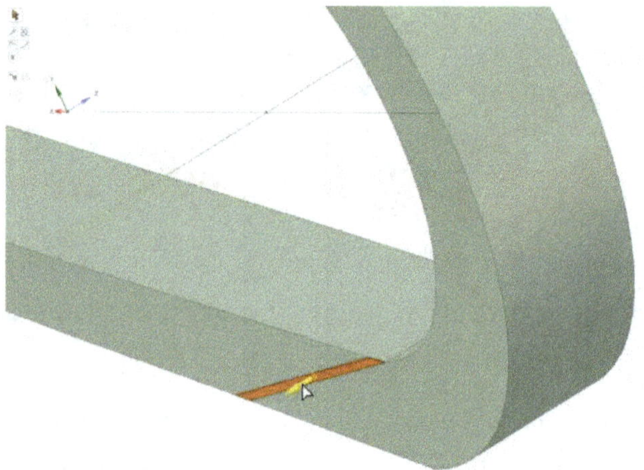

Figure 36: Creating the section for the snap hook's opening in 3D mode

Finally, we will round a few edges using "Pull". You can freely choose the rounding radii according to your preference.

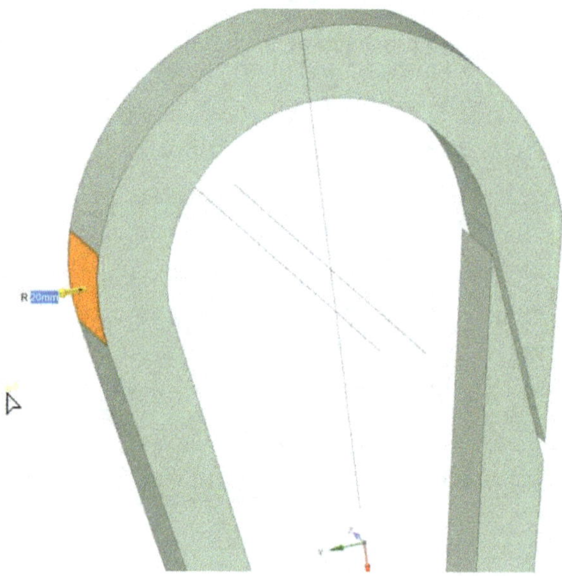

Figure 37: Rounding some edges of the carabiner

7.2 Design project theory: "Modify"

Awesome! Before we move on to the next design project, let's make another brief theoretical lesson. For the 2D sketch of the carabiner, we got familiar with "Trim away" from the section "Modify". There are a few more helpful features in this section. I would like to briefly introduce them to you in the following. For this purpose, I have prepared a few geometric elements. Using "Create Rounded Corner" you can easily and quickly create a rounded corner. Select the first line, enter the desired radius, and then select the second line. The program now creates the desired rounded corner.

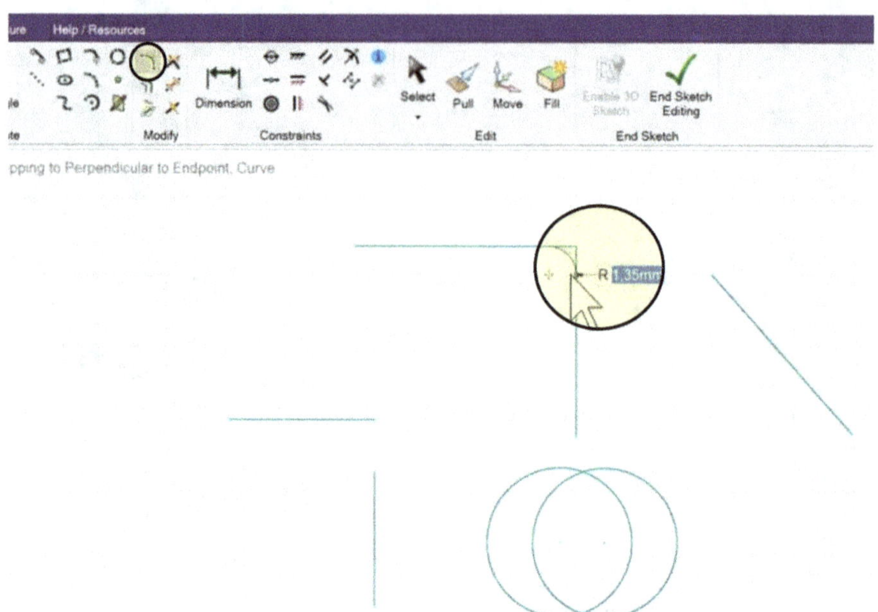

Figure 38: Create rounded corner function from Modify (Sketch menu tab)

With the feature "Create Corner" you can create a corner out of two independent line elements. Simply by selecting the two lines. One or both lines are extended or shortened so that a corner is created.

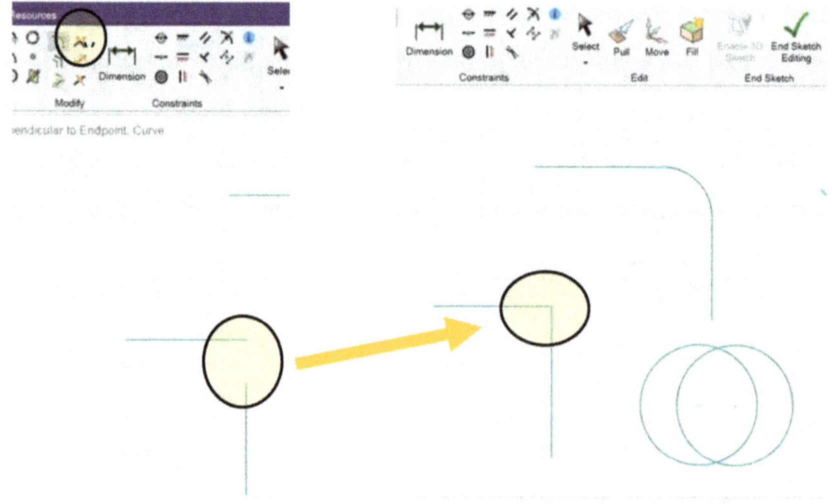

We already had the function "Trim away". With this, you can remove superfluous line segments.

Finally, let's take a look at "Split Curve".

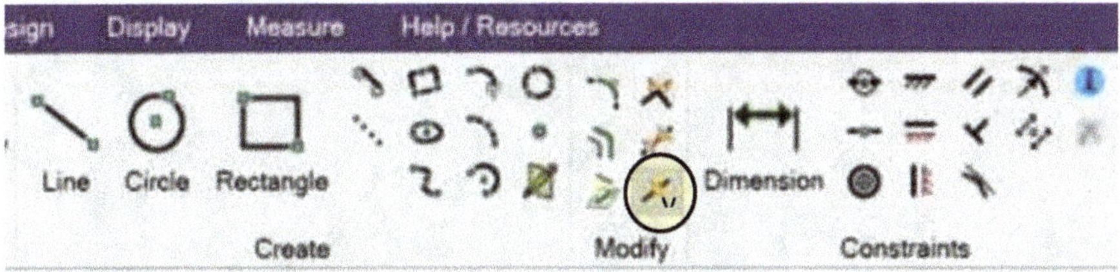

We can use this if we want to split an element, such as a line, at a certain point. Select the line and specify a point. You will see that the line will then be split into two lines at that point. If we delete the existing condition (right-click on the line and then select the red X), we can better see where the split point is and move the separated lines.

8 Design project # III: Mounting Component

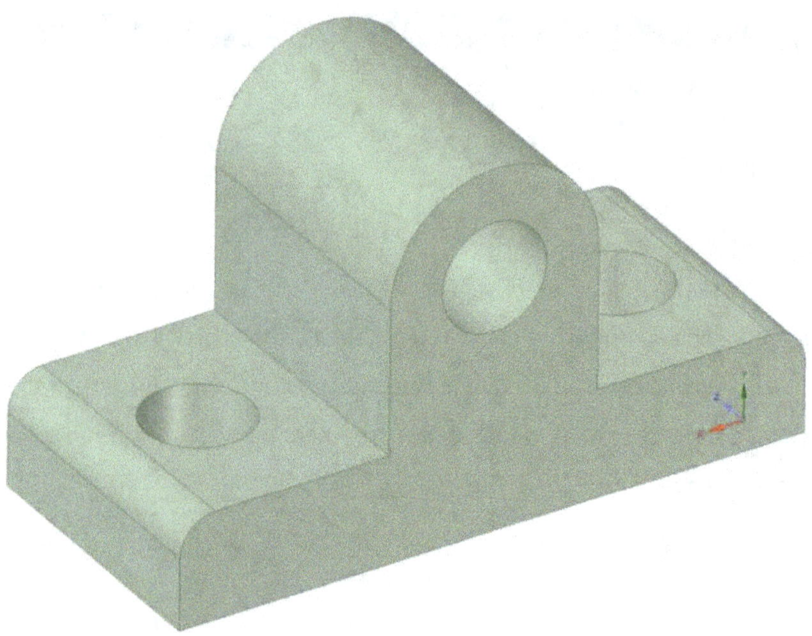

The next design object is a simple, fictitious mounting component. It can be attached using two bolts and is used, for example, to hold an axis or another turned part.

We start by drawing the cross-section of the part in the 2D sketching environment. You are welcome to pause the course at this point and try to create the 2D sketch completely on your own.

A tip: Draw the front side of the object. You can choose the dimensions freely. Extrude it afterwards with "Pull".

Alternatively, you can proceed with the book and simply try it afterwards.

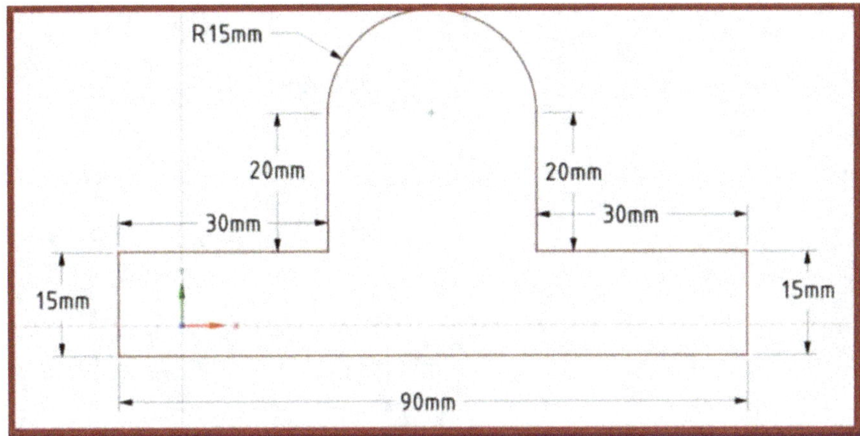

Figure 39: Dimensions and geometry for the mounting component

First draw a baseline of e.g., 90 mm and then two side lines with 15 mm height and 30 mm width each.

Figure 40 First steps / lines for the 2D geometry of the part

Then we need a part of 20 mm height, and finally, we use the function "Tangential Arc" to create a semicircle. After selecting the function, click on the two upper ends of the drawn profile, and you will see how the arc is created. Afterwards, you can define the radius of the arc with e.g., R = 15 mm.

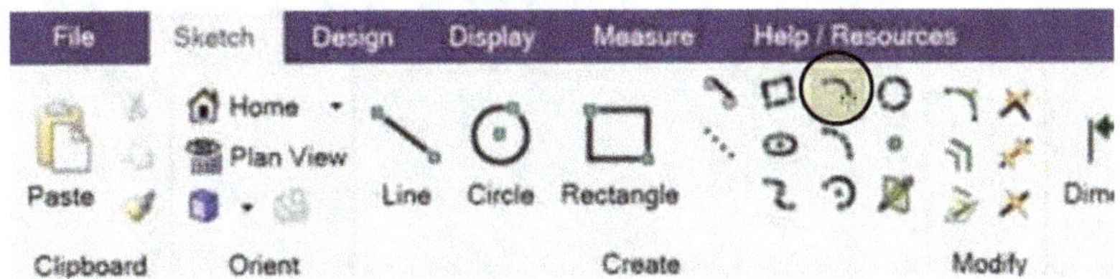

Figure 41: Function "Tangential Arc" to complete the sketch

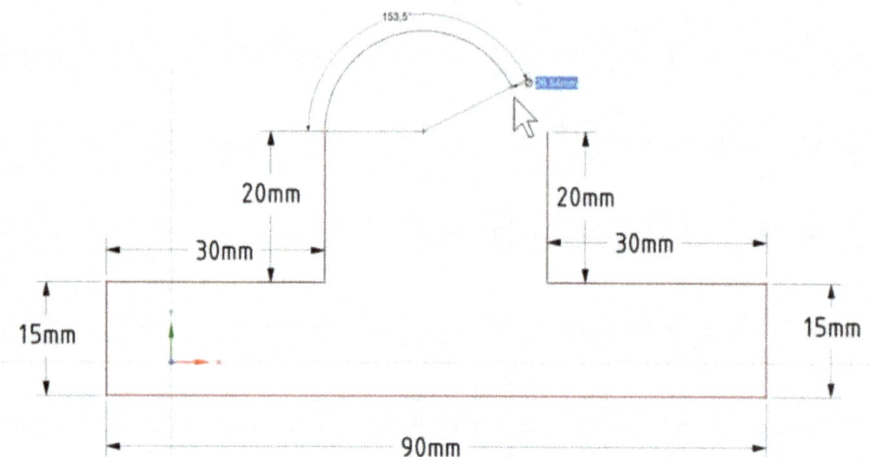

Figure 42: Completing the sketch for the mounting component

Then, as usual, use "Pull" to get a 3D object. You can use 40 mm, for example.

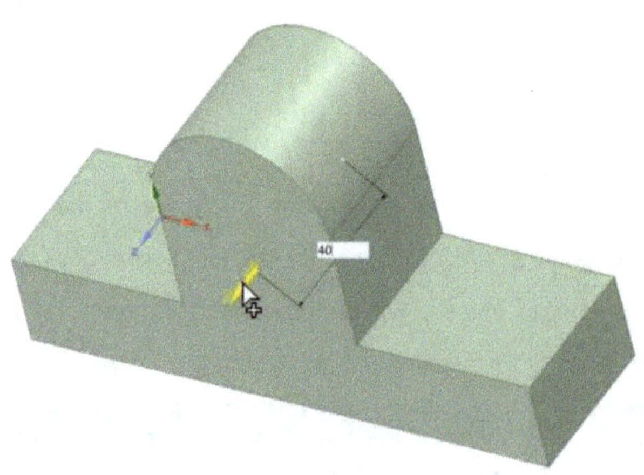

Figure 43: Pulling the 2D surface into a 3D part

In the next step, we will create the drilling in the upper part of the component. To achieve this, switch back to 2D sketch mode and select a suitable view. For example, the front face of the object.

Next, draw a circle with a diameter of 15 mm on the starting point of the upper semicircle. Alternatively, you can simply draw the circle and set it concentric to the semicircle using a constraint.

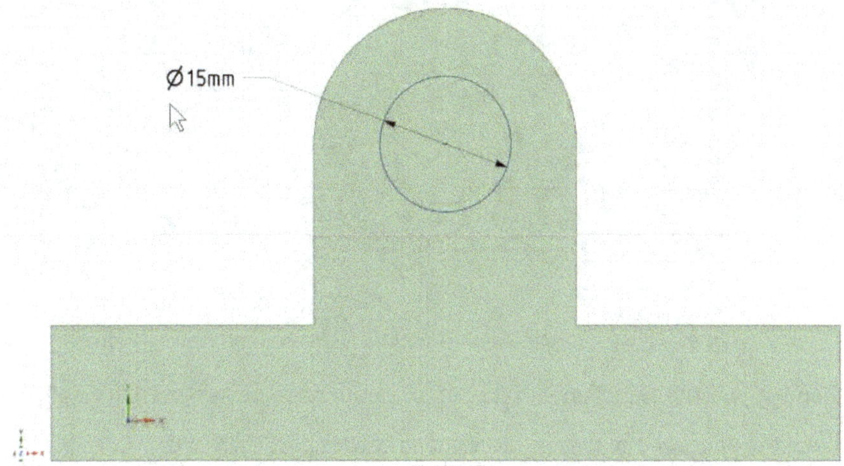

Figure 44: Creating the circle geometry for the hole on the front side

You might also notice that you could integrate this step right into the first 2D sketch. Great!

When the sketch is done, the drilling can then be executed by "pulling" it in 3D mode.

For the two mounting holes, switch back to the 2D sketch environment and select a view that allows you to look at the component from above, i.e., preferably the top view. Then draw two guide lines on each of the two surfaces of the component between the centers of the edges of these surfaces.

Thanks to these guide lines, we can perfectly position two circles with diameters of 15 mm in the centers of the surfaces without further dimensioning. Alternatively, you can simply dimension from the center of the circles to the side lines.

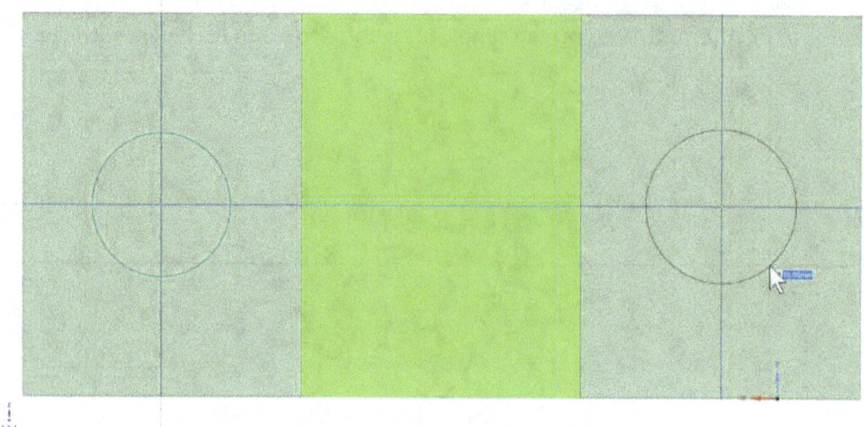

Figure 45: Circular geometry and auxiliary lines for the holes on the side surfaces

Then we pull the sketched surfaces in 3D mode to remove material. Finally, we round the edges of the two surfaces and finish the part in this way.

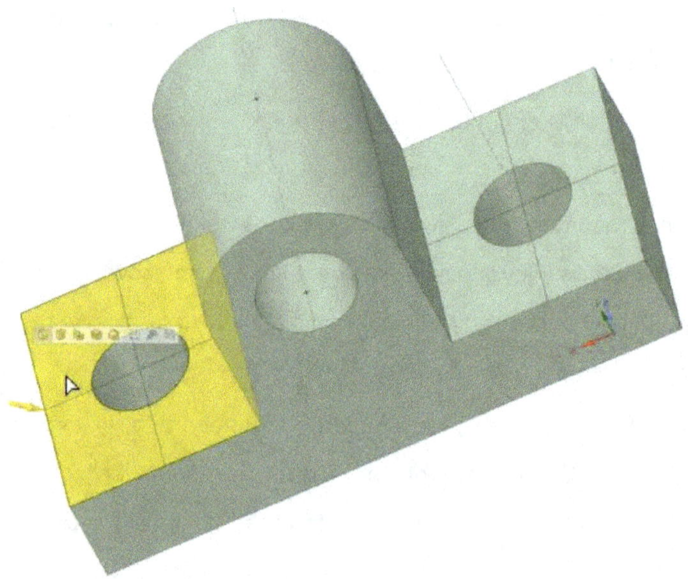

Figure 46: The part is almost finished. Edge rounding is missing

9 Design project # IV: Smartphone Stand

In this chapter, we want to create a smartphone stand. You may have to adapt the dimensions to your smartphone.

Let's start with a 50 mm long and horizontally aligned line on the y-z plane. To do so, we must first select the correct view ("z" must point upwards and "y" must point to the right) and then select the button "Select New Sketch Plane" in the lower area.

Figure 47: "Select new sketch plane"

Then we click on the displayed view. But why are we drawing on this specific plane? We use the y-z plane so that at the end the views "Isometric", "Top", "Bottom", "Left", "Right", etc., are displayed correctly. Because we are drawing the cross-section or the side surface of the smartphone holder on this plane. Just look at the part from the side, then you will understand what is meant. We will draw the side surface, which is shown here so that we can extrude the 3D element.

Figure 48: Sectional view of the stand; we need to sketch this surface

If you don't understand it straight away, you can sketch at any other plane and then click through the views, and you'll understand.

Let's start with a 50 mm long and horizontally line (1) on the y-z-plane.

Then we'll add a 20 mm line at 45 degrees (2) and a 23 mm line at 35 degrees (3). Followed by a 3 mm horizontal line (4) and another 16 mm line (5), which should be parallel to the second line drawn. Continue with a 10 mm horizontal line (6). By the way, you can easily switch between the input field for the dimension and the field for the angle using the tab key.

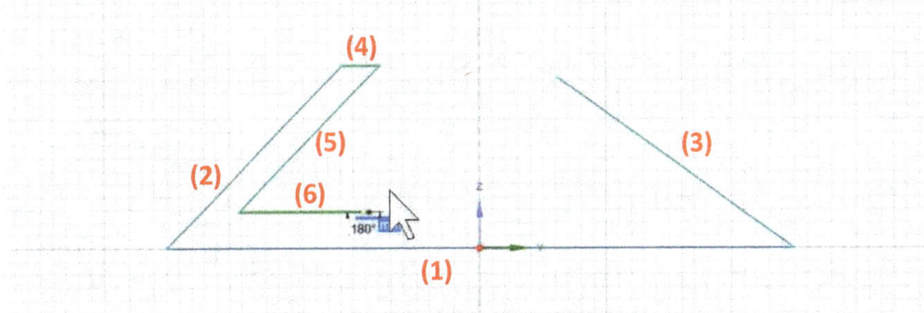

Figure 49: The first lines of the 2D geometry

Now we have to create the support surface for the smartphone. To do this, we draw a 85 mm line at 135 degrees (7), a 5 mm horizontal line at the top (8) and another connecting line to complete the profile (9).

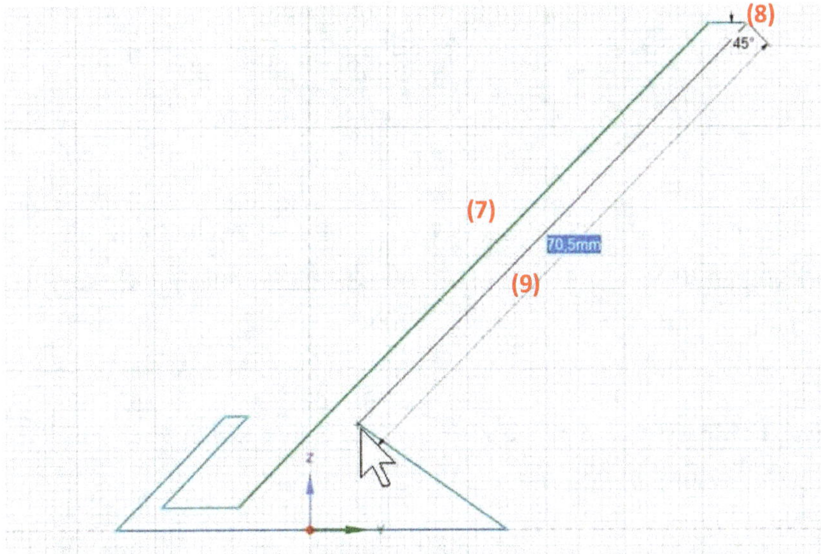

Figure 50: Completion of the profile

Now the cross-section profile is done, and we can switch to 3D mode and create the three-dimensional model using the well-known "pull" function. We need 50 mm.

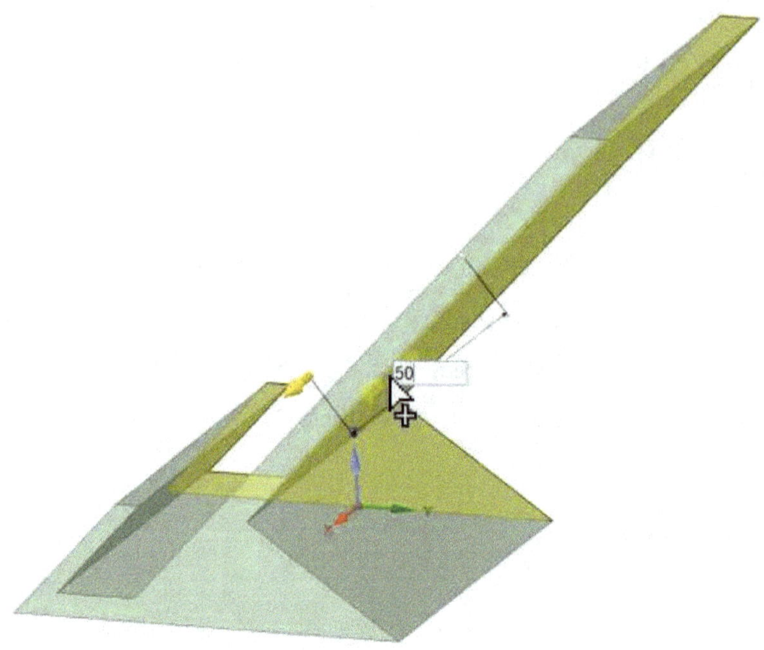

Finally, we round a few edges as follows: 2 mm at the front bottom, 1 mm at the back bottom. 2 mm for the rest. Of course, you can also round other edges if you want to!

That's how easy it is to create a simple smartphone stand! Great job! Please continue with the next chapter.

10 Design Project # V: Bowl

In this section, let's take a look at an object that seems a bit more complex to create: a bowl. How can we start? For example, we could begin by drawing two circles on two different planes and then connecting them. Alternatively, we could design it as it would be machined (by turning). But more about that later.

First, let's go the more complex way, using planes in order to get to know a new feature. For the bottom of the shell, we'll first use a simple circular geometry. Start in 2D sketch mode and draw a circle with a diameter of 70 mm.

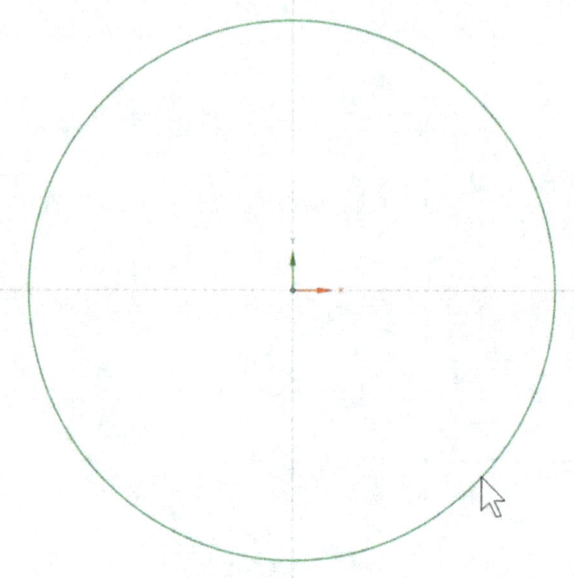

Figure 51: Sketch a 70 mm circle on the x-y plane

For the top of the bowl, we create – in 3D mode – an additional plane by selecting the "Plane" function, which you can find in the "Design" section, and by clicking on the previously created circular area.

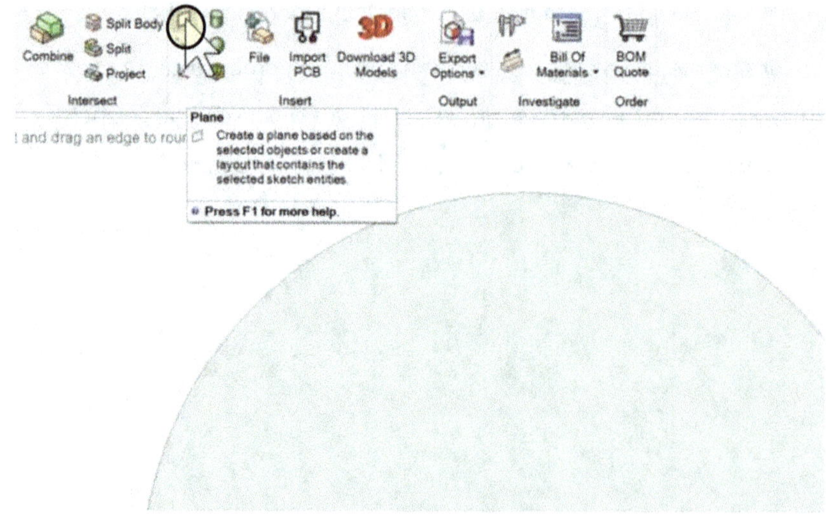

Figure 52: Create a new plane

Now we select the created plane and move it with "Move" in the direction of the z-axis (blue coordinate arrow). Enter a value of 80 mm.

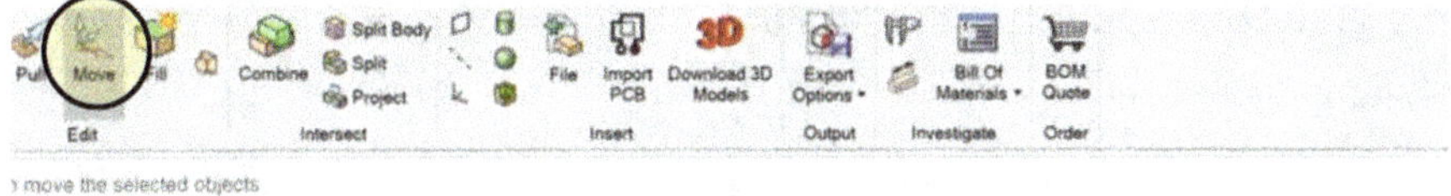

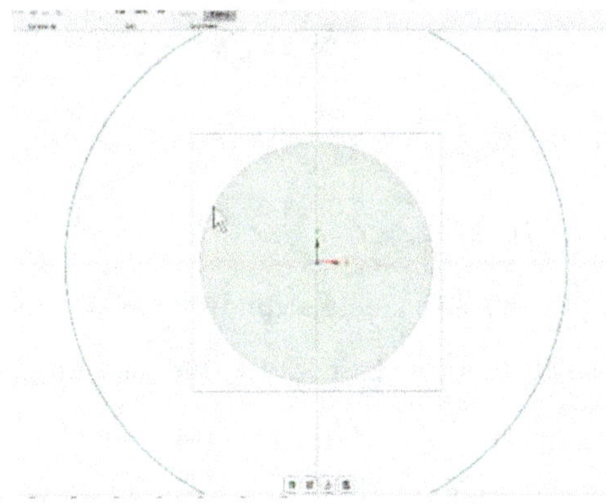

Figure 53: Move created layer (light blue) with "Move"

Next, start a 2D sketch on the newly created plane and switch to "Top view". First select the plane and then draw a circle with a diameter of 150 mm in the center of the coordinate system.

Figure 54: Create a circle with 150 mm diameter on the new plane

Make sure you are in 2D sketch mode for this step and that you have selected the correct plane.

Then we switch back to 3D mode and select the two circle surfaces – holding down the CTRL key – and select the "Blend" or "Fill and Connect Surface" feature at "Design" and "Edit".

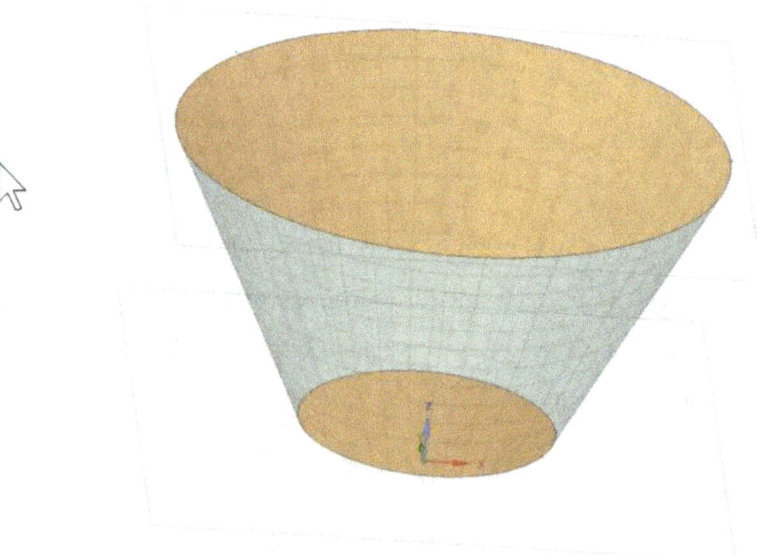

Figure 55: Apply "Blend" feature to get a cone

The program uses this feature to create a cone-shaped fill area between the two selected faces. Quite convenient, isn't it? By the way, by right-clicking on the selected plane and choosing "Hide", you can – if you want – hide the created layer.

With this feature, we got a solid cone. For the bowl, however, we need to hollow it. Therefore, select the "Shell" feature and click on the top surface of the created object. Select a wall thickness of e.g., 5 mm. Almost done!

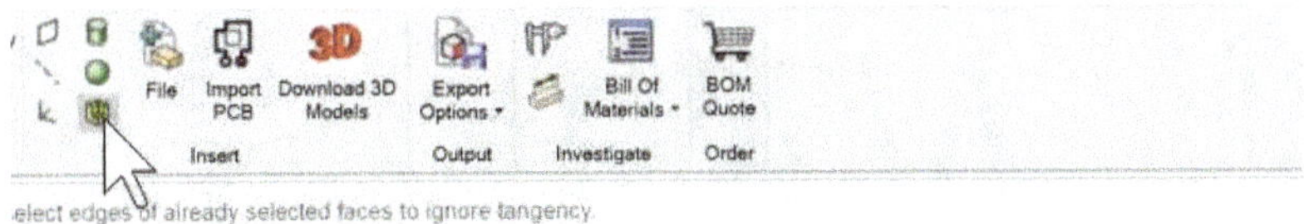

Figure 56: Apply Shell function to obtain a hollow cone

Finally, we can make some edge roundings to improve the design. For example, as follows: Let's use a radius of 2.5 mm for the two top edges of the bowl and a radius of 10 mm for the edge of the bottom of the bowl.

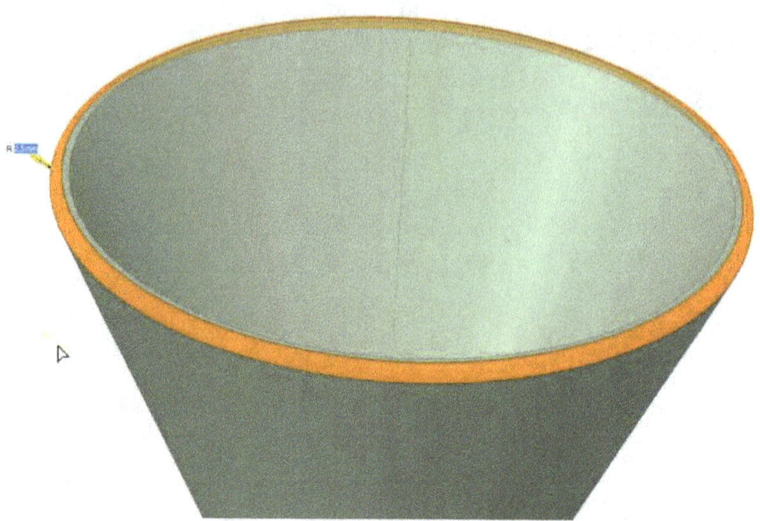

Figure 57: Apply edge roundings to the hollowed cone

Let's try the simple way. As mentioned at the beginning of the chapter, we can also design the bowl as it would be machined.

We would do this as follows: We first draw a vertical guide line on the x-z plane, which will later serve as an axis of rotation.

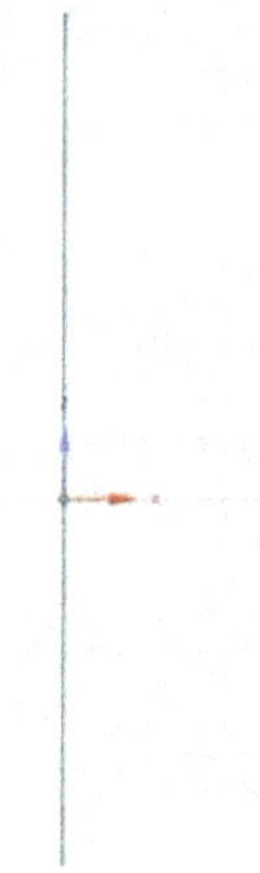

Figure 58: Vertical auxiliary line for rotation; length can be freely chosen

Now imagine that we would cut through the bowl from above. We would get two halves of the bowl.

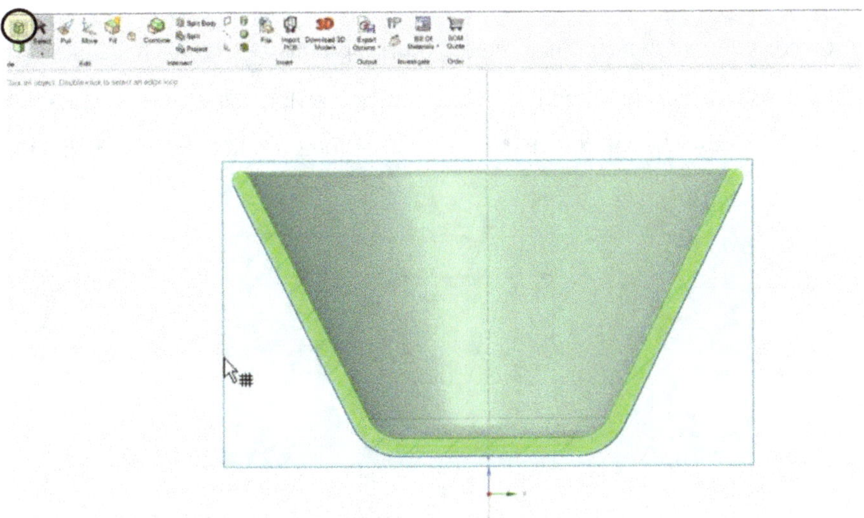

Figure 59: Section view of the bowl

<u>Note:</u> To obtain the section view of a component, you must first create a plane by selecting the "Plane" icon and selecting the z-axis. Then select the "Section mode" function and select the previously created plane. The program will now create a section view.

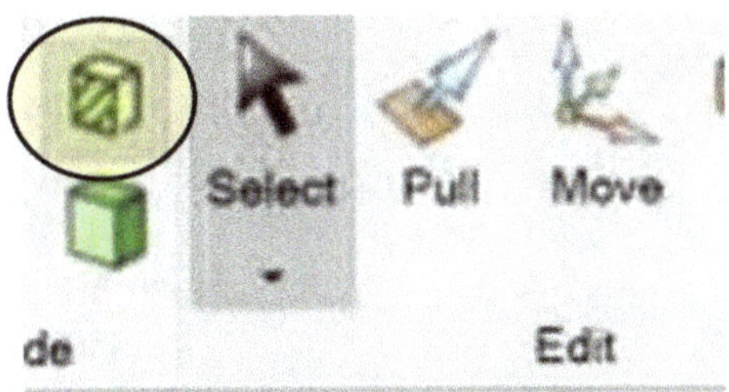

Figure 60: "Section mode" to create the section view

We have to draw this cross-section on the x-z plane, to rotate a complete bowl from it later. We use the x-z plane because we want to see the front of the cross-section when drawing it. By the way, we draw without the rounded edges. We simply add them at the end. Let's just try this, then you will surely understand what is meant.

For the cross-section, we draw a baseline of 35 mm, which is half the width of the bowl at the bottom. Then we draw the wall of the bowl and dimension the top distance as 75 mm, which is half the top bowl width. Since the wall had 5 mm, we want to use that value here as well. We're only drawing half of the cross-section profile, since we'll be rotating that half by 360 degrees around the z-axis to get the full bowl.

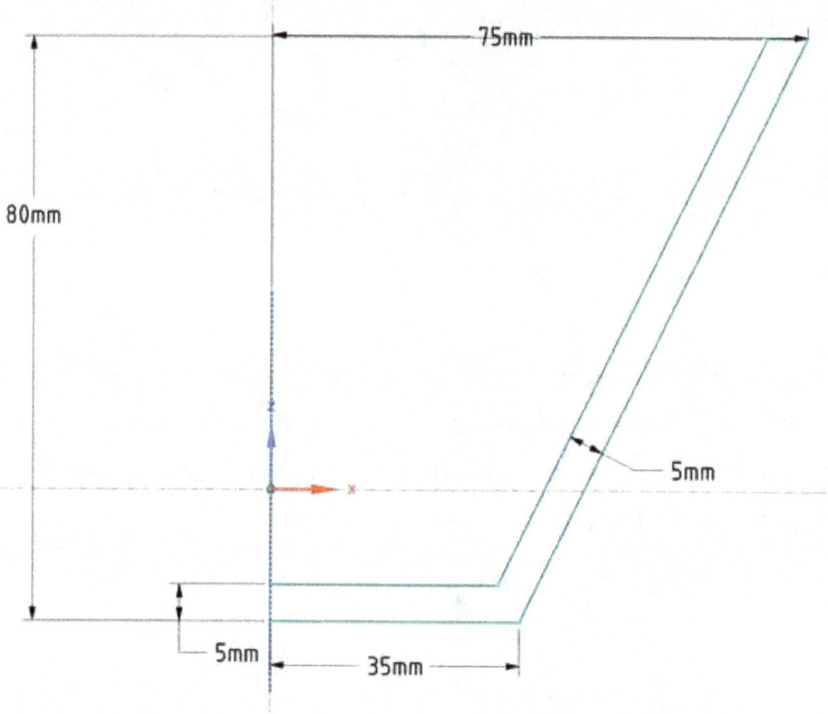

Figure 61: Geometry and dimensioning of the cross-section sketch (half)

After we have completed the sketched profile with another line, we can rotate it around the rotation axis by selecting the "Pull" function and by selecting the option "Revolve" in the upper-left corner.

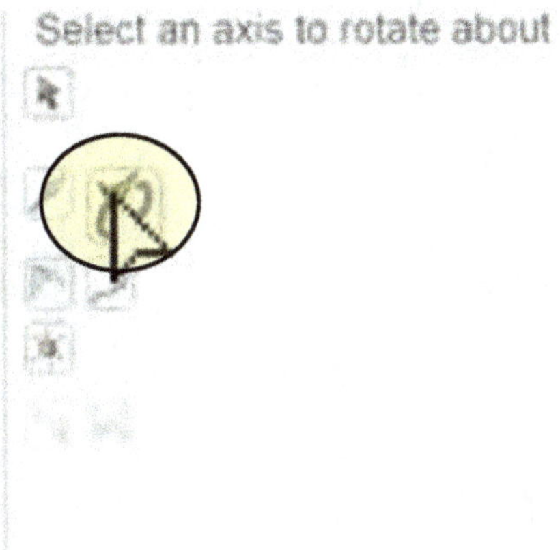

Figure 62: Selection of "Revolve" in the upper-left corner after selection of "Pull"

First, select the rotation axis, i.e., our guide line in the z-direction. In the second step, select the drawn surface. For a complete rotation, we need to enter 360 degrees.

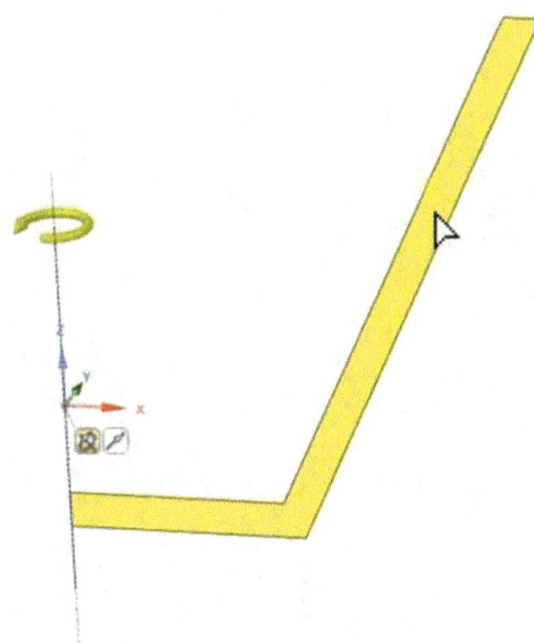

Figure 63: Selection of the surface and axis to start a rotation

This way we get the bowl in a quick way.

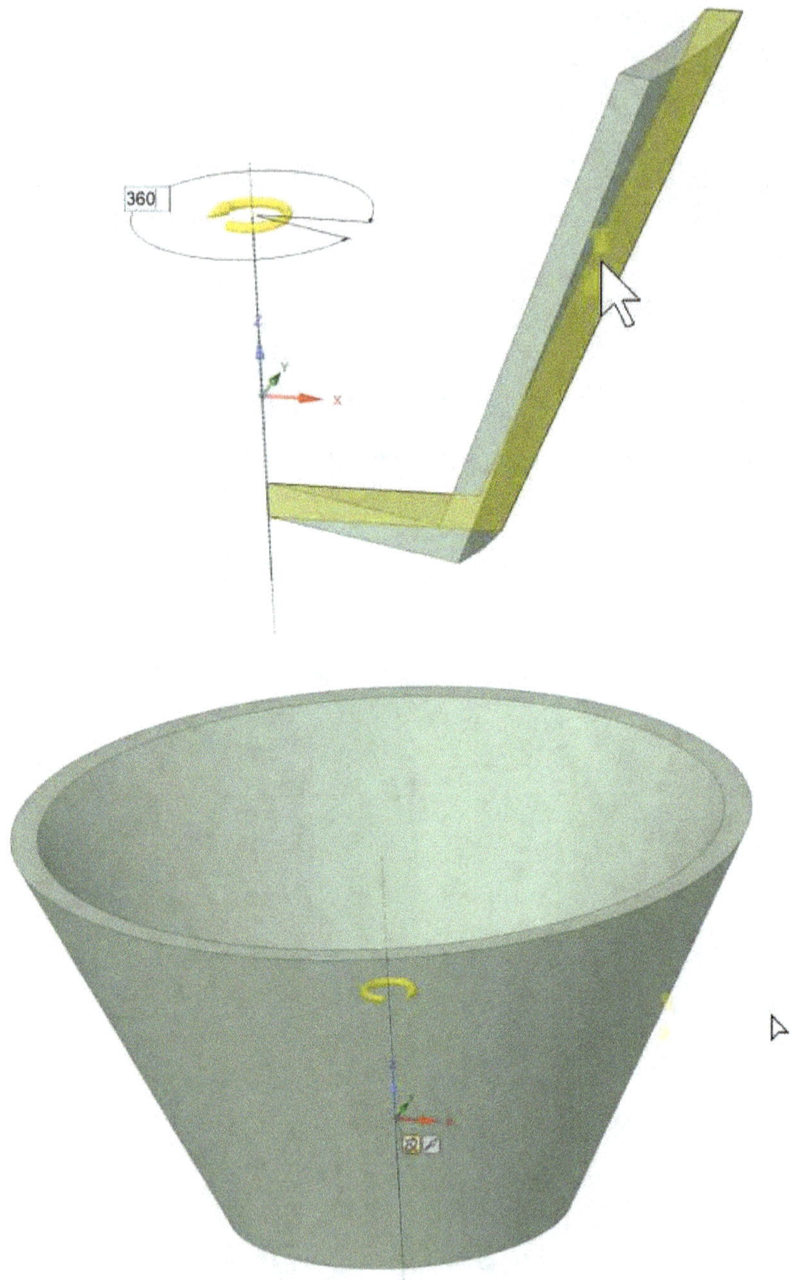

Figure 64: Rotation of the bowl and finished bowl (360°)

As a last step, you could round the edges again. You can see that there are several possible ways to the same goal, as already mentioned in the beginning.

Depending on which one you choose, you will be able to design faster and/or easier. If you design something every now and then, you will develop a sense for the fastest and easiest method after a while. Let's keep going! The next project will be a cup!

11 Design Project # VI: Cup

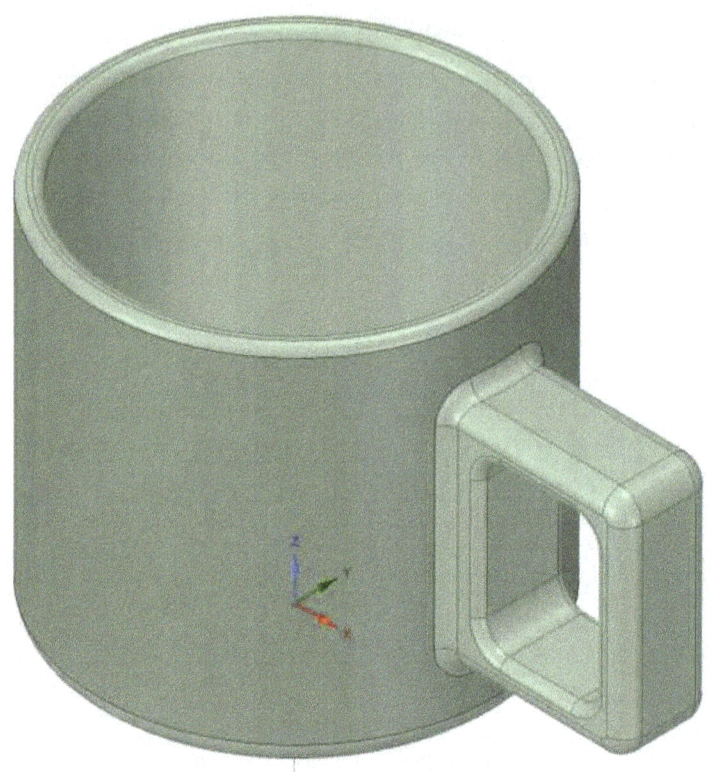

Next, we would like to design a cup including a handle. In the following, attempt to pay attention to the combination of additive and subtractive design methods. Start a new project and create a circle in the 2D sketching environment. The diameter could be 90 mm, for example.

Then switch to 3D mode and create a cylinder from the sketch using "Pull". A dimension of 80 mm is used here. Then utilize "Shell" to hollow the cup. We select a wall thickness of 5 mm.

e to shell without removing a face.

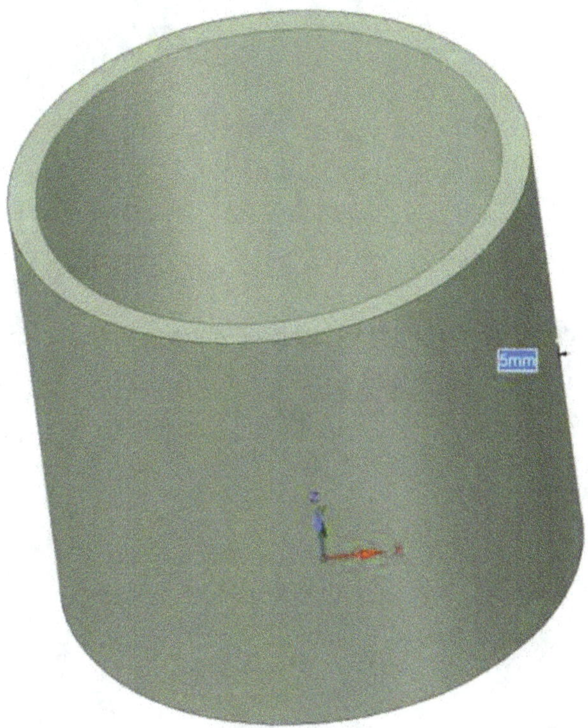

Figure 65: Cylinder element for the cup: draw a circle (90 mm), use "Pull" (80 mm) and hollow it with "Shell" (select upper surface; 5 mm wall thickness)

In the next step, create a new plane for the handle of the cup on the surface of the upper cup rim.

Then move this plane 15 mm downwards, i.e., in negative z-axis direction. This is done by selecting the plane and moving it using the blue z-axis.

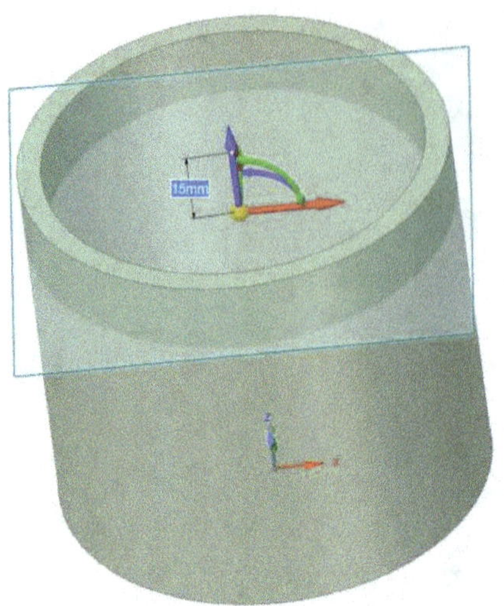

Figure 66: Create a new plane (on the mug's rim top) and move it downwards

But, why do we do this? Because the handle should not be on the same level as the edge of the cup, but a little bit lower.

Then select "2D Sketch" and "Top View" to create a vertical line of 20 mm on the previously created plane.

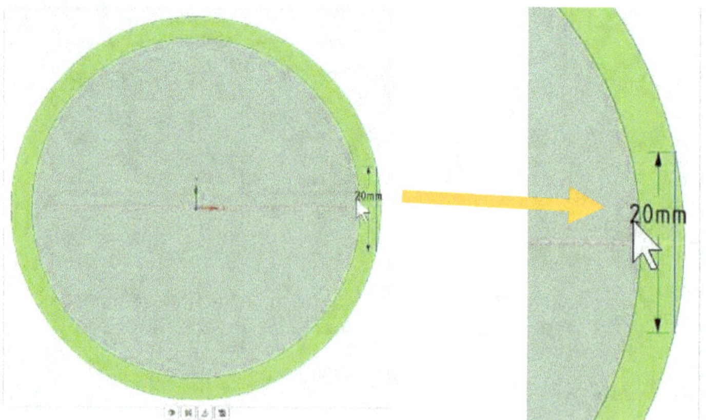

Figure 67: Create a 20 mm vertical line

Complete the profile with 2 horizontal lines of 40 mm and a vertical one, so that a rectangle is created. Now, you can probably already guess the shape of the handle. In this case, the element is added to the basic cylindrical element, i.e., the cup.

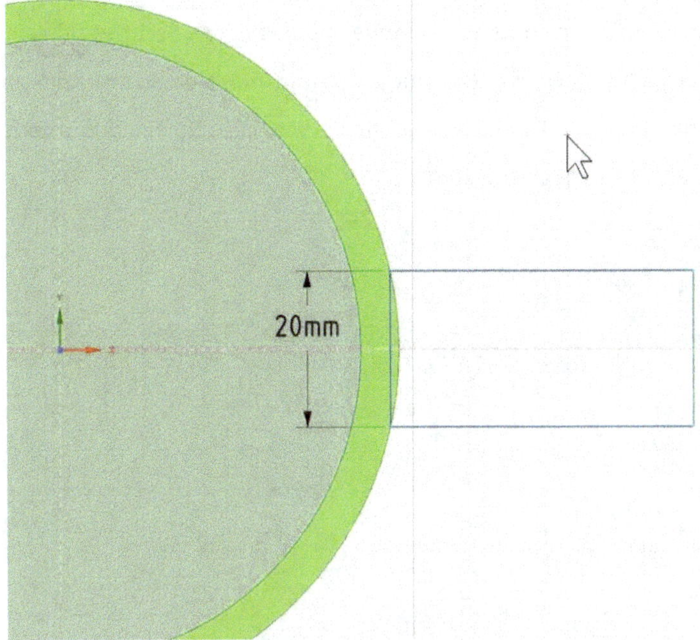

Figure 68: Add two horizontal 40 mm lines and one vertical line

In 3D mode, you can create the handle by pulling it downwards, that means in negative z-axis direction. We choose a dimension of 50 mm.

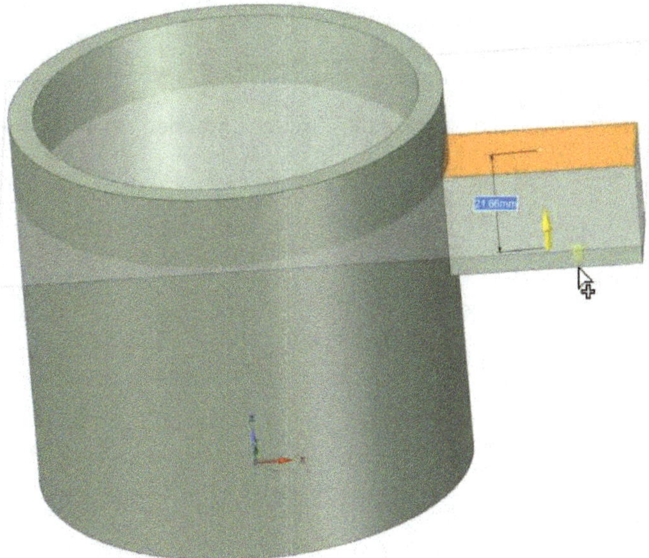

Figure 69: Create the basic shape for the handle (50 mm dimension)

In the next step, switch back to 2D mode and this time select the side surface of the handle as the drawing plane. Draw a 26 mm wide and 36 mm high rectangle from a center point, and add the dimensions 20 mm and 25 mm. Alternatively, you can work with guide lines as well.

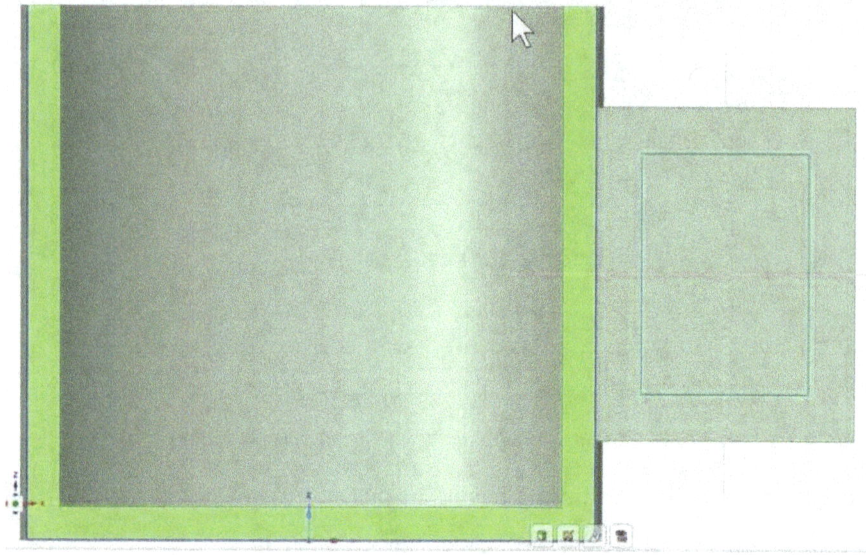

Figure 70: Sketching the cutout for the handle

Then you can make the cutout in 3D mode. Finally, we round some edges of the handle and the cup and try to display a few other renderings of the cup.

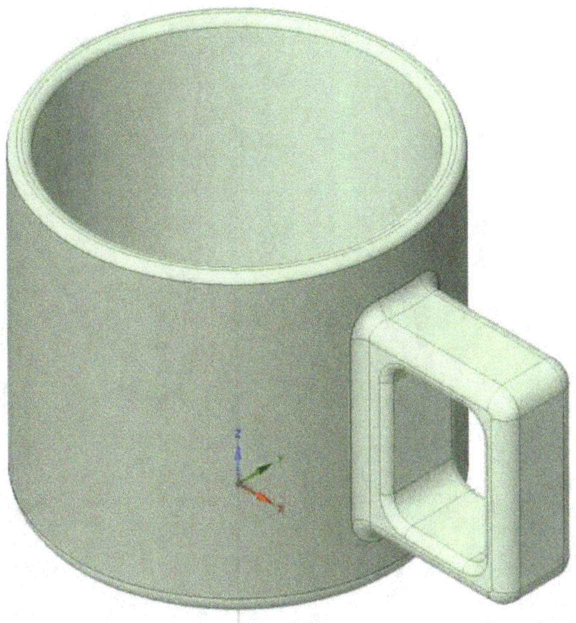

Figure 71: Finished cup with handle

Switch to the section "Display" for the selection of "Graphics" and try out a few renderings.

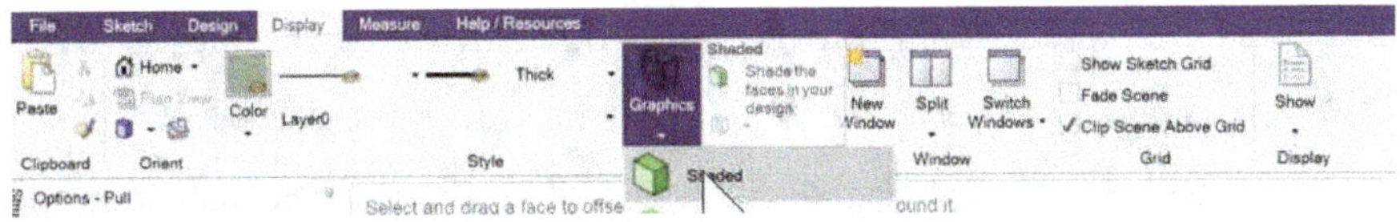

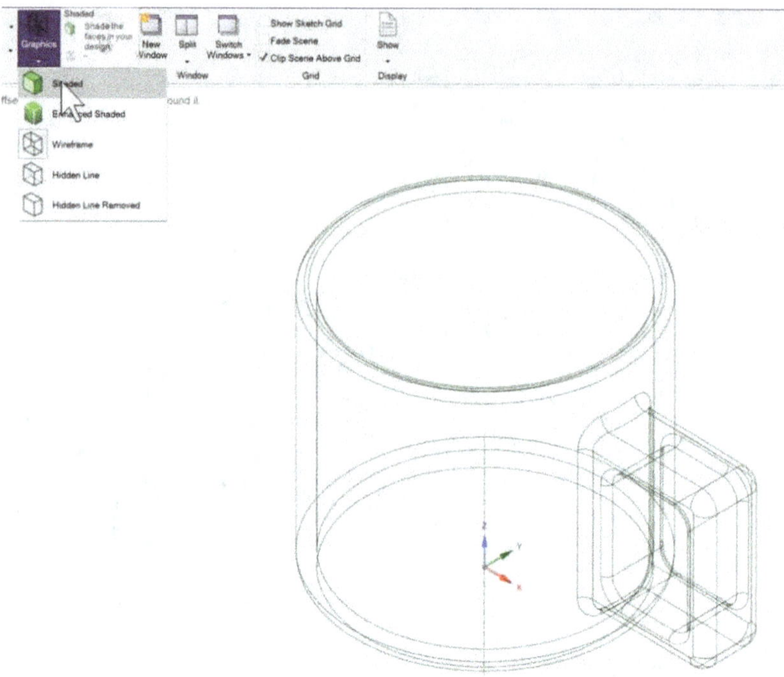

Figure 72: Alternative renderings of the cup

As a final project, we will create an internal thread for a square nut in the following chapter. This thread could even be 3D printed and is fully functional.

For a bolt, the thread creation would work similarly. In this chapter, however, we will draw an internal thread instead of an external thread. By the way, threads can also be created automatically with the help of other CAD programs, such as Fusion 360 from Autodesk. If you have made it this far, you can be proud of yourself because you have learned all the basics as well as all important functions and approaches for working on further projects!

12 Design Project # VII: Square nut (Thread)

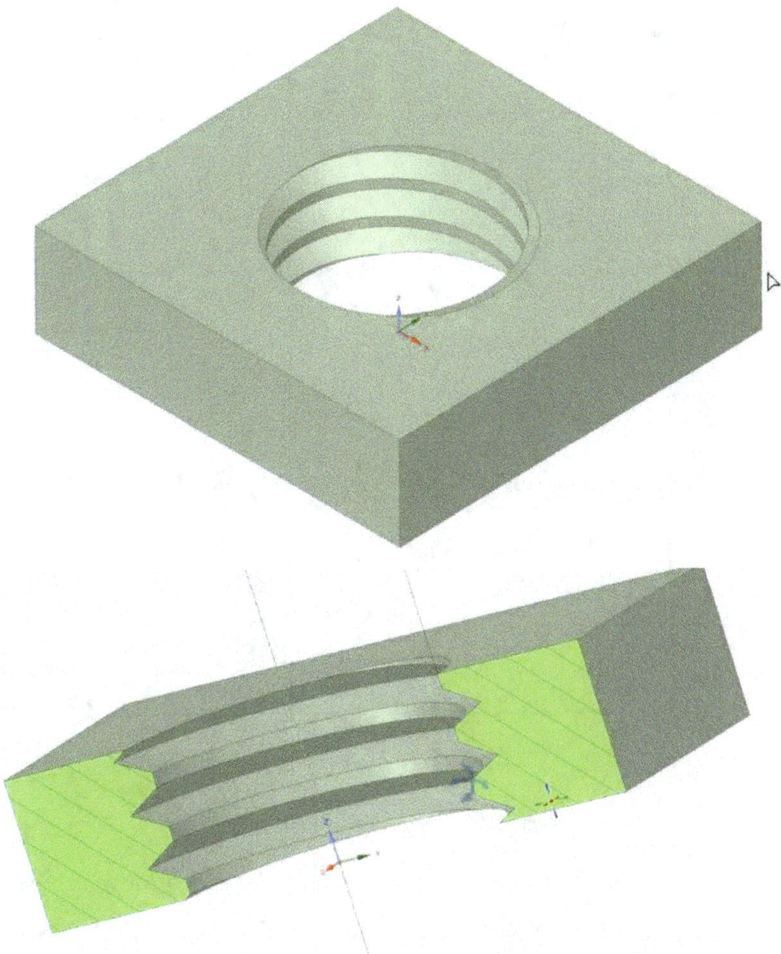

For the square nut with a thread, we create a rectangular part in the 2D sketching environment with a width of 20 mm and a height of 20 mm.

Complete the profile with a circle. Then, select the diameter d = 10.2 mm. The dimensions for standard parts of mechanical engineering, such as bolts and nuts, can be found in an engineering book or even easier: by googling.

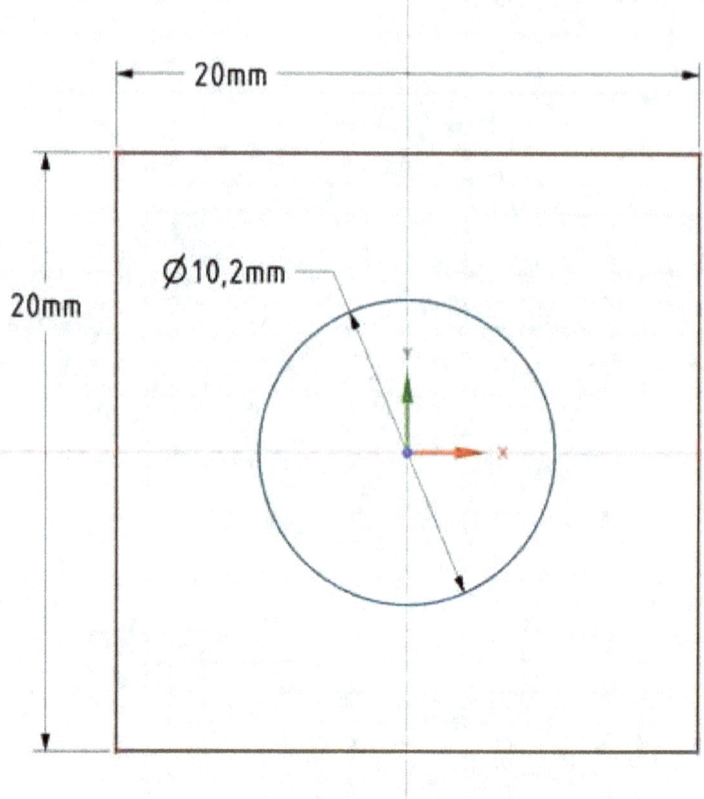

Figure 73: 2D sketch of the square nut

After creating the sketch, switch to 3D mode and "pull" the area between the circle and the square into a 3D object. Use a dimension of 5 mm. You can delete the circular area then.

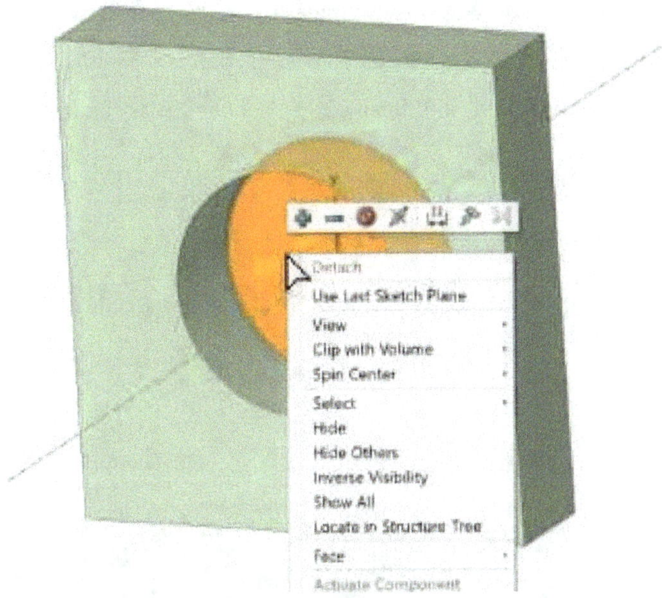

Figure 74: Create 3D part and delete circular surface area
(right click on orange surface, then "Delete")

Next, select "Section Mode" and select the y-z plane of the part by clicking on the z-axis. We are now in the section view.

In this view, create two vertical guides as follows using the 2D sketching mode. The distance between them should be 1.14 mm.

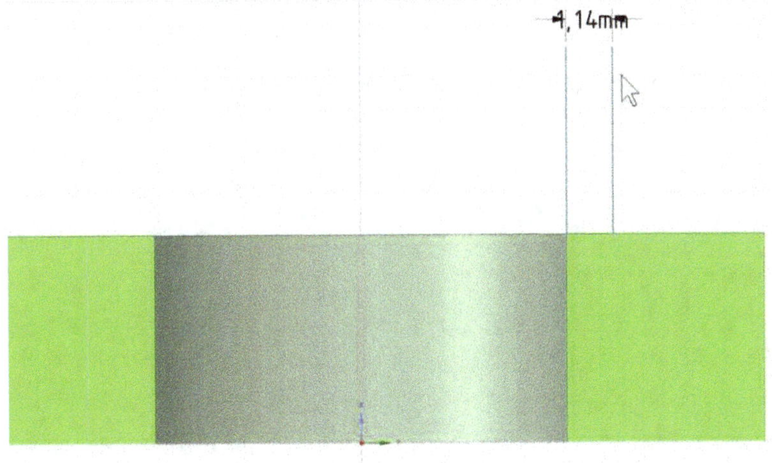

Figure 75: Creating two guide lines in the section view

In the next step, we draw a small triangle. To do this, first draw a connecting line at 30 degrees between the two guide lines (1). Then another line at 60 degrees in the opposite direction (2) and finally a vertical line (3) as the last element of the triangle.

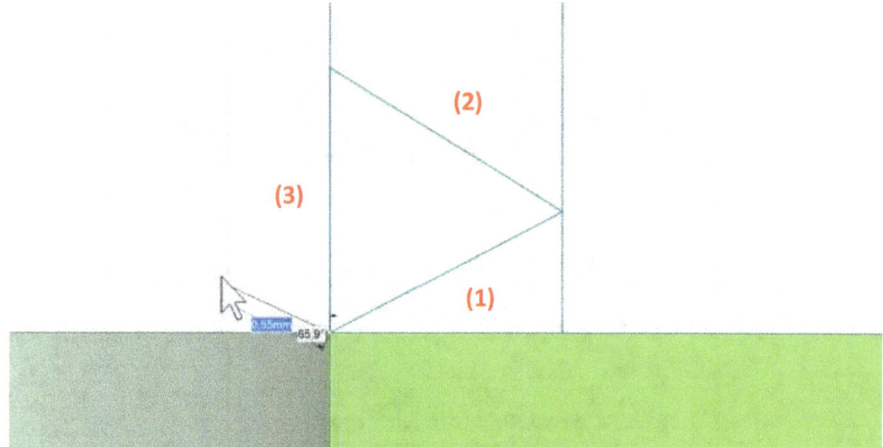

Figure 76: Create a triangle between the guide lines

We need this triangular profile to create the thread. The dimensions and angles for the particular thread can be obtained from an engineering book or the Internet. In our case, we draw an M12 internal thread.

To create the thread, we switch to 3D mode and select the triangular surface. Then we click on "Pull" and use the feature "Revolve", which can be found in the upper-left corner. The next step is to activate the option "Cut" and "Revolve Helix" in the sidebar at "Options".

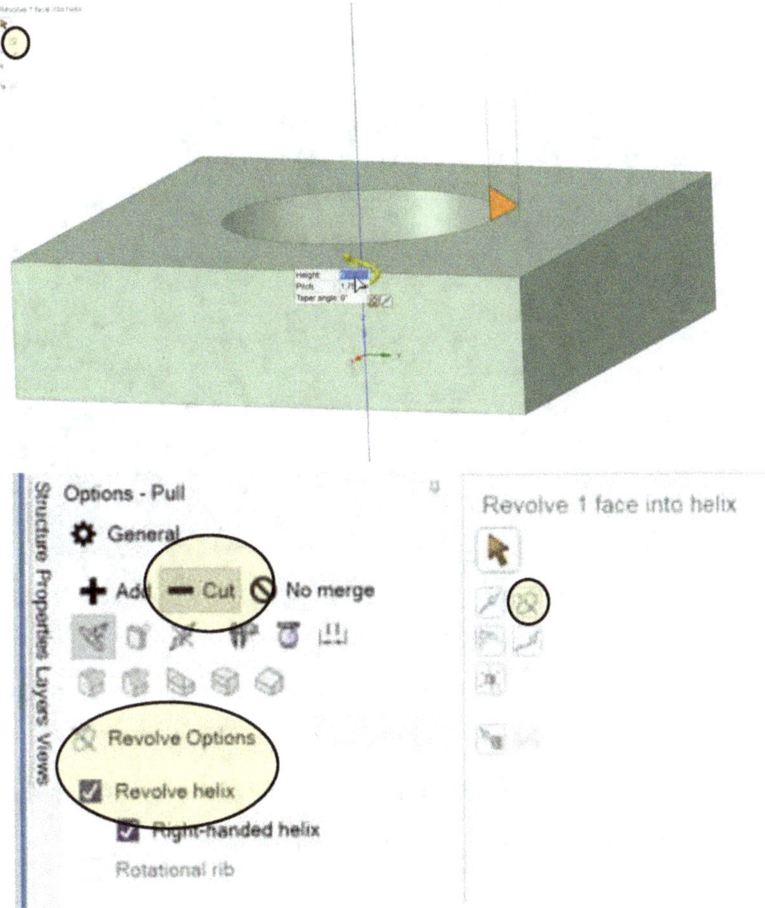

Figure 77: Rotate the triangle profile with "Revolve" and select options

For the rotation of the thread, select the z-axis, i.e., the axis of the drilling, as a rotation axis. After selecting the axis, we have to activate the function "Revolve helix" in the left sidebar under Options. A small box appears. Here, as a last step, we enter the values "Height" (e.g., -15 mm), "Pitch" (e.g., 1.75 mm) and "Taper Angle" (e.g., 0), which we also get from an engineering book or online.

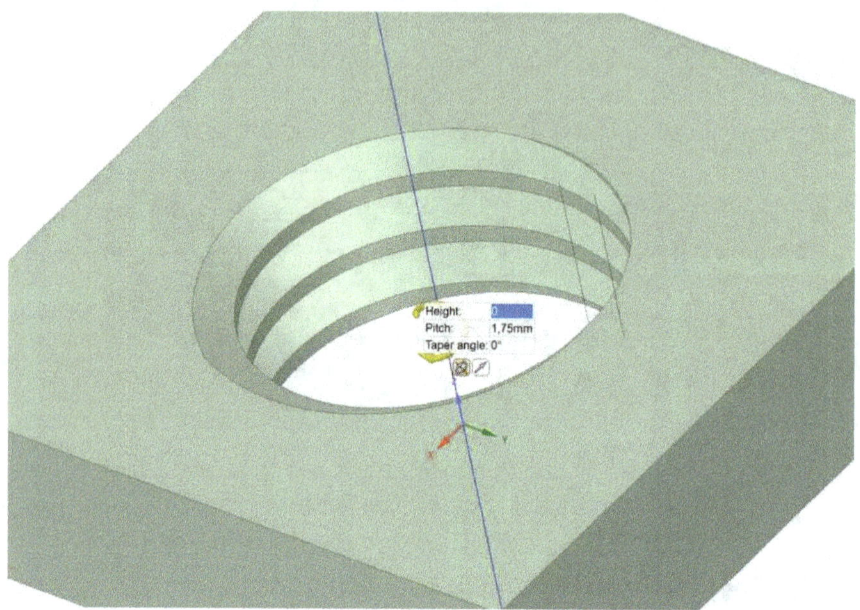

Figure 78: Enter values for thread creation

As a result, you should get such a thread. Finally, you can save the project. Choose a "DS Mechanical File" to edit the file later.

Alternatively, you can also use the "stl" format to create a file for a 3D printer with a slicing software. Perfect, threads are no problem anymore!

13 Closing Words

This brings us to the end of the course. But now it is time for you to think about some new design projects, to consolidate the methods you have learned and to improve them in this way. Be creative with the projects! You have learned all relevant operations in the 2D and 3D mode in this course. This enables you to design your own CAD files in a quick and easy way.

And as mentioned at the beginning of the course, please also take a look at 3D printing. It's tremendously fun and beneficial to materialize your designs.

This way you have a solution for all sorts of unavailable but much needed spare parts or anything else. Take a look at my book: 3D Printing 101 | The Ultimate Beginner's guide and get your copy right away on amazon.com. Thank you very much and have fun with further designing!

Please write a short review if you liked this book! It would mean a lot to me and will help all other design newbies!

Thank you very kindly!

Books on topics you might also like

All books are available online on the usual sales platforms. It's best to just search for the title, or feel free to visit my author page. Some of the books may not be published yet and will be released or found soon. Take a look at the books of your choice and your copy as e-book or paperback!

3D Printing:

CAD, FEM, CAM (3D Object Creation, Design, Simulation):

Electrical Engineering:

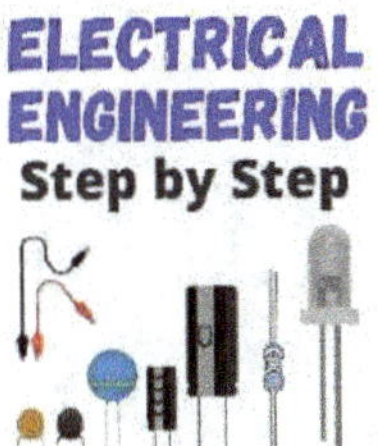

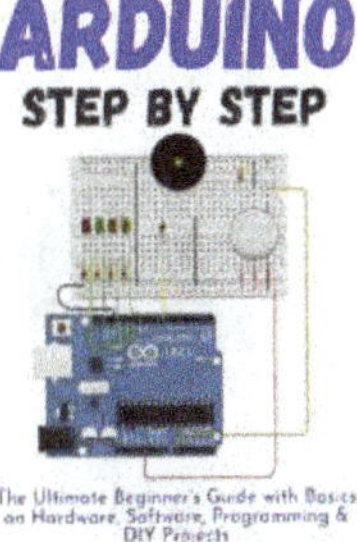

Programming and other Software:

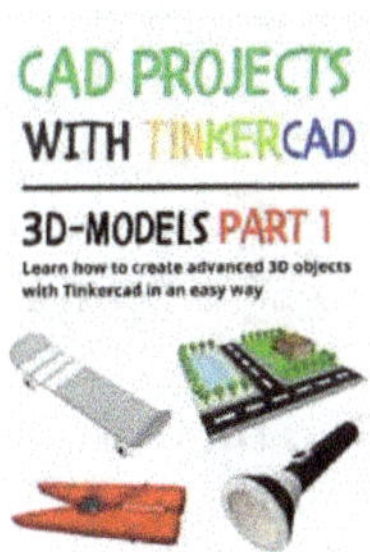

There are also identical video courses for some of these books:

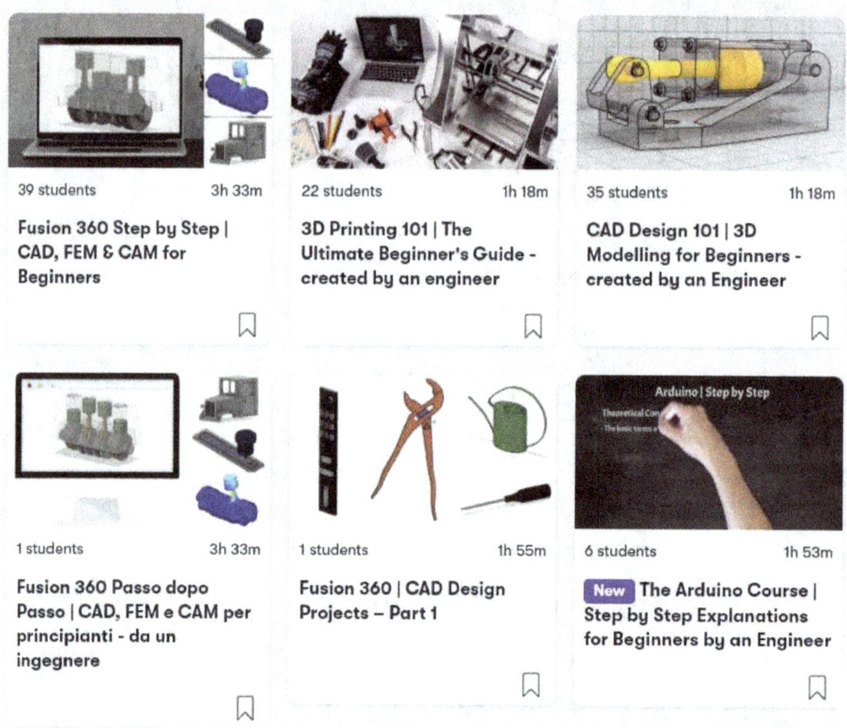

They are hosted on the learning website: skillshare.com

Be sure to use my following friends & family referral link to get a month of membership for free !

(I will get a little bonus if you choose to stay, so we will be both 😊 Thanks in advance!)

https://www.skillshare.com/r/profile/Johannes-Wild/854541251

It is best to copy the link in your browser to access the free month !

Sign up today and deepen your knowledge!

Imprint of the author / publisher

© 2023

Johannes Wild
c/o RA Matutis
Berliner Straße 57
14467 Potsdam
Germany

Email: 3dtech@gmx.de

This work is protected by copyright

Thank you so much for choosing this book!